Crewel
intentions

Crewel intentions

Fresh ideas for Jacobean embroidery

HAZEL *Blomkamp*

SEARCH PRESS

ACKNOWLEDGEMENTS & THANKS

Louise Grimbeek, Sandra Kloppers, Pat van Wyk, Penny Woolridge and Margie Breetzke for 'proof stitching' the designs in this book and pointing out my typographical and content errors;

Darren Willson, Louise Grimbeek and Pat van Wyk for keeping the business running whilst I indulged in the creative process of putting this book together;

Wilsia Metz and fellow authors Di van Niekerk and Trish Burr for the long telephone conversations that all add up to friendship and support. We'll do Paris again together girls!

And to my husband Peter and son John who, along with their love and support, have both become competent and creative cooks. They've had to. It's the only way they are guaranteed a meal at night.

First published in Great Britain 2014
Search Press Limited
Wellwood, North Farm Road,
Tunbridge Wells, Kent, TN2 3DR

Originally published in South Africa in 2014 by Metz Press, 1 Cameronians Ave, Welgemoed 7530, South Africa

ISBN 9781782211068

Publisher   Wilsia Metz
Design and layout   Liezl Maree
Proofreader   Carla Masson
Illustrations   Wendy Brittnell
Photographer   Ivan Naudé
Reproduction   Color/Fuzion
Print production   Andrew de Kock
Printed and bound by TWP Sdn. Bhd., Malaysia

Contents

Introduction

The joy of working with a Jacobean shape is that it is a blank canvas waiting to be filled with, well, whatever you like really.

Traditionally worked with wool on linen twill, crewel embroidery has endured since the 17th century. Along with the desire to recreate the classic shapes typical of this style of embroidery, needle artists have enjoyed working with these fanciful fruits and flowers for hundreds of years. For the most part, though, stitchers have stuck to tradition, using crewel wool and working only with those stitches that are to be found under the heading, Crewel Stitches, in any and every Stitch Gallery.

In this modern era with its wide choice of yarns, fabrics, fibres and beads there can be no reason to be stuck in a rut, working only with materials that have been used for the last four centuries. They have served their purpose. It's time to move on.

Coupled with this, one has to consider that in an era of instant communication through the internet, a technology that provides an exchange of ideas that has never happened in human history, the time is surely ripe to break through barriers. Barriers that have previously dictated that embroiderers should not mix techniques and styles.

This book sets out to show you how to take Jacobean or crewel embroidery to another level.

Not a shred of wool has been used, only cotton, rayon and metallic threads, along with beads and crystals. The designs in this book are embroidered onto cotton, linen, taffeta and silk – not twill – and the techniques, whilst making full use of crewel embroidery stitches, borrow from other styles and other needle crafts. Needle lace techniques, Brazilian and bead embroidery stitches, stumpwork techniques and last of all loom weaving methods have been incorporated into the embroidery that fills the Jacobean shapes in all of the designs.

In some cases these techniques have been used unchanged and in others – in particular the needle lace and loom weaving methods – have been tweaked and converted to fulfil their new roles as embroidery stitches. They provide variety and banish boredom.

All of the projects have been mounted in objects that will make them useful additions to the home. Should you wish to mount your projects in the same way, I have provided a Buyer's Guide at the back of the book. As each item is from a reputable craft dealer, you will find the links to their websites on this page.

I hope you will enjoy the new ideas in this book and that it will take you on an interesting and satisfying journey.

HAZEL *Blomkamp*

General tips

YOU MUST BE ABLE TO SEE PROPERLY

One of the most common inhibiting factors for embroiderers, especially those of a certain age and older, is being able to see properly. This is of particular importance when one is doing fine work. Optometrists' machines are set to magnify at about waist level. This does not work for embroidery because you will generally hold your work at chest level. When you visit your optometrist, take a piece of your work with you so that your spectacles can be made to suit your working style. The best spectacles are bi-focals with the bottom part of the lenses made to magnify, by two or three times, at chest level.

You may have to insist and, in the process, promise your optometrist that you won't sue him if you fall down a flight of stairs. Failing that, just bully him into giving you what you want. He will then take away his expensive machinery and place a pair of old fashioned frames on your nose, so that you can hold your work at the right level while he puts different combinations of lenses into the slots. If everyone is concentrating and you shout stop when you can see your stitches perfectly, you will end up with one pair of spectacles that works for everything, except walking down stairs. Alternatively, you can have a separate, dedicated pair of needlework spectacles made in the same way.

Since I wrote the above suggestions in *Crewel Twists*, I have got older, my eyes have got weaker and my work has got finer. So, I am going to give you yet another tip.

Having persuaded your optometrist to give you the right spectacles, if you are working on something really fine, like the weaving in some of the designs in this book, you then need to go off and buy yourself a pair

of 'off the peg' reading spectacles with a strength of 1 to 1½ – no more than that or they will be too strong. When you are stitching, wear these in front of your prescription spectacles thereby creating a telescopic effect. It really works and is more comfortable than grappling with magnifying glasses that hang around your neck. A word of warning though. Because this whole arrangement is so comfortable you may forget that the second pair is on your face and answer the door, or drive to the supermarket looking silly. Remember to take them off when you don't need them.

If, however, you are younger than I am, you can ignore all of the above. And if you are older, I have no suggestions. Yet.

GOOD LIGHT

No matter what your age and the state of your eyes; you should always embroider in a well-lit environment. You don't want to have to restrict yourself to only being able to work during daylight hours, so you will need a good light. My favourite light used to be an ordinary metal lamp with a 100-watt bulb. However, for some reason, it has become almost impossible to buy reading lamps that will accommodate a 100-watt light bulb.

Most lamps have plastic fittings and can only take a 60-watt light bulb. This is not bright enough and if you put a 100-watt bulb into these lamps, the fittings will burn up. So, the best is now a 50-watt halogen light. Most good halogen lights come with two settings – 35 and 50 watt. Don't be persuaded to buy a cheap and nasty one that only emits 35 watts. It's not bright enough. Working under a halogen lamp can be hot, particularly in summer, so have a fan blowing onto you and try not to worry about your carbon footprint. It can't be much worse than if you were doing machine embroidery.

KEEP YOUR FABRIC TAUT BY WORKING IN A HOOP

This improves the tension of your work and stops the fabric from puckering. The best are good quality plastic hoops. They are less inclined to break, give a better grip on the fabric; thereby holding the tension required for better stitching and, because dogs seem to prefer the taste of wood, are less likely to be chewed.

- The first option is a hoop with an inner ring that has a lip at the top. If you use it properly, the lip on the inner ring creates a 'dog leg', which means that the fabric does not loosen. If you like to work 'hands free', use a hoop stand. If you don't want to have to buy another cupboard to house your hoops, the best stand to use is one that has a clamp, on an adjustable arm. This will accommodate any hoop size.
- The next option is a no-slip hoop. Available either separately or together, with struts that hold them together to form a lap stand, these hoops have a groove on the outside of the inner ring and a ridge on the inside of the outer ring which fits into the groove. This stops the fabric from slipping once you have tightened the screw. The lap stand option is

very useful if you like to work 'hands free' and it can be disassembled for storage.

- I try to choose a hoop that accommodates the size of my design, so that every line is visible. Sometimes, because of its shape or size, a design requires a square or rectangular hoop. Until recently, this has been difficult because there was nothing that gripped the fabric as tightly as I wanted it to. Recently, however, a little number with teeth has come onto the market and it works beautifully. At first it seemed a little flimsy, but then I realised that was part of its charm. Once you have assembled it to the shape you want and stretched your fabric over the teeth, the fabric helps to keep the whole thing together and what seemed to be flimsiness translates to the lightest frame you will ever use. Easy to hold and manipulate.

Every person has his or her hoop preference and I have listed mine. You may have hoops and frames that you prefer and you should, of course, use those. All that is important is that you do use a hoop or frame and that you remove the fabric from the ring when you are not working, so that your finished product does not end up with a permanent crease.

MAKE A FABRIC GUARD

No matter how often you wash your hands, you have natural oils that will be deposited on your embroidery while you are working. Add to that the problem of drinking coffee and eating chocolates while you are working. I have an additional problem, one that – I suspect – applies to many others. If one of my droopy-faced dogs gives me a plaintive look while I am stitching, I am going to pat him. I might even give him a rub and a tickle, which is going to make my hands a little grubby. I keep a pack of hand wipes on my stitching table and I do wipe my hands regularly, but I refuse to become obsessive about it.

If your threads are colour-fast, none of this is a problem because you will be able to wash your work once it is complete – more about that later. However, almost without fail, a grubby ring will form at the place where the fabric meets the outer ring of the hoop, and sometimes it won't wash out, no matter what you use. To avoid this problem, make a fabric guard.

Cut a square of fabric (poly-cotton sheeting works well) that is about 15 cm (6") larger, all around, than the hoop that you are using. Find a round object that has a diameter that is about 6 cm (2½") less than the diameter of your hoop. I usually use a dinner or side plate. Place it in the centre of your square of fabric and draw around it. Cut out the inner circle so that you end up with a square that has a round hole in the middle. To use the fabric guard, place it over your embroidery fabric with the working area exposed. Make sure that the hole in the guard is approximately in the centre. Place the outer ring in the normal way. Roll the outside edges of the fabric guard around the embroidery fabric that is not inside the hoop and pin them together on the underside with curved safety pins.

If you neaten all the raw edges with zig-zag stitch or an overlocker, you will have a fabric guard that lasts for years. I have one for each size of hoop that I own.

USE TALCUM POWDER ON YOUR HANDS

Our grandmothers used to put talcum powder on their hands when they were knitting and that was a very clever thing to do. Even if you use a fabric guard, those pesky natural oils on your hands will still cause problems, particularly if you are stitching with white thread on white fabric. Dipping your fingers into a bowl of baby powder every time you re-thread your needle absorbs anything that is left after you have washed and dried your hands. You may be left with a residue of powder on the embroidery, but this will rinse out, unlike the grimy spots left by your fingers, which won't disappear, no matter what potion you use.

KEEP YOUR THREADS TIDY

The best way to do this is to wind the threads onto cards and keep them in the plastic storage boxes made to hold floss cards. I have heard arguments against this method, but it works better than anything else I have found. If the cards cause kinks in your thread, run them through a thread conditioner before you thread them onto the needle.

UNPICK

Don't leave bad stitching and untidy work where it is. Others may not be able to spot your mistake, but you will always know it is there and will never be satisfied with your finished project. If you find that unpicking is demoralising, don't do it straight away. Move onto another section of the embroidery and come back to the unpicking when you can face it.

USE A THREAD CONDITIONER

It strengthens your thread, makes silk and rayon threads less lively and delays the stripping of metallic thread. Bees wax is good, but the best is a silicone thread conditioner. This leaves no residue.

THREADING NEEDLES

The best way to thread a needle is to 'needle the thread'. Snip the thread with a sharp pair of scissors to get rid of any fluff, tightly squeeze the threading end between the thumb and forefinger of your left hand (right hand if you are left handed) leaving only a very small tip showing, make sure that the eye of the needle is facing upwards and slide it over the thread. It works every time.

USE SUPERGLUE

I don't like using a thimble but find that a hole develops in the tip of the finger that I use to push the needle through the fabric. Murphy's Law dictates that on every third stitch, the back of the needle will go straight into that hole and the pain will cause me to go straight through the roof. I place a blob of superglue on that spot, hold my finger in the air for a few minutes and let it dry. Once that blob is dry it will be rock hard and a needle will not penetrate it. It peels off after a few hours. I promise. It's only in cartoons that superglue victims have to be taken to the emergency room with glasses stuck to their foreheads.

START YOUR STITCHES WITH A KNOT

Yes, a knot. This is the 21st century. We do embroidery for our pleasure, not to be judged. Whilst the back of your work should not look like a bird's nest, it no longer has to look the same as the front, particularly if it is going to be displayed in a way where the back will never be visible.

UNTANGLING A KNOT

Use two needles to untangle a knot. Your fingers are too large to do the job.

TAKE IT SLOWLY

Some embroiderers can work quickly and, at the same time, maintain a high standard of work. Most can't. It's not a race and if you work at the speed of a train going somewhere in a hurry, like the passengers, your work will end up scattered and bent. The pleasure of embroidery is in the journey, not the destination. Focus on the pleasure of working a small area without worrying about the bigger picture.

ARM'S LENGTH PLEASE

As an embroidery teacher of many years' standing, I find that it is more difficult to teach a perfectionist than a mere mortal. Whilst embroidery involves the pursuit of perfection, one has to accept that anything that is hand-made will inevitably have imperfections. Whilst stitching, one is necessarily focusing on a few square inches and sometimes one has to hold one's work away from oneself in order to be objective. You should work the stitches to the best of your ability but you make it so difficult for yourself if you try to be perfect. If it looks good from arm's length, then it is good.

TRANSFERRING YOUR DESIGN

The line drawings for all of the designs in this book are at the back. The easiest way to transfer them onto your fabric is with dressmaker's carbon. I know there are all sorts of more acceptable methods that involve the pricking of paper and using powders, or using a lightbox and pencil. But, like most things in life and embroidery, I do what works best for me. And dressmaker's carbon, or chalk paper, is my choice.

- Make a photocopy of the drawing, adjusting the size where recommended.
- Pin the photocopy to the fabric, taking care to place it in the centre and with the grain of the fabric. Don't get too fussy about the grain. You're not doing even-weave embroidery so just get it as straight as you can.

- Place a sheet of dressmaker's carbon, ink side down, between the photocopy and the fabric.
- Using the hard tip of a ball point pen – preferably one that has no ink in it (I have a dry pen in my tool box for this task) – go over each and every line pressing hard. And I do mean pressing hard. You should end up with a sore finger. If you don't press hard enough the lines won't transfer.

Another alternative is to pin the photocopy to the underside of the fabric. Place it on a light box and trace the lines on with a pencil or a tailor's pen.

And if the above is all too much for you, order a print pack from our website!

WASHOUT TAILOR'S PENS

The blue washout pen has been around for a long time and, more recently, a white one for use on dark fabrics has become available. I use both of them and I love them. They glide smoothly over the fabric, making it very simple for me to alter any lines that I have decided to change. Where I have transferred a drawing onto fabric with chalk paper and the lines have rubbed off, they are the perfect tools for drawing the lines back into the design.

They are, however, controversial because they have caused brown lines that, for some needlecrafters, won't wash out. Brown lines and stains will be avoided if you follow two simple guidelines. Always rinse your embroidery in cold water before putting it into any detergent; and, do not allow the lines to fade. If you draw something onto fabric with a washout pen, grow bored with it and put it away in a cupboard for a while, when you come back to it those lines will have faded to brown and you won't get rid of them.

Provided you avoid the two points mentioned above, you can use a washout pen with impunity. It is the easiest way to draw something onto fabric.

WASHING YOUR EMBROIDERY

I can understand why, in the 17th century, it was not a good idea to wash a piece of embroidery on completion. Our forebears did not have colour-fast dyes and fabrics were inclined to shrink. It is now, however, the 21st century and technology has moved on to, not just satellite dishes and the internet, but colour-fast dyes, non-shrinking fabrics, gentle bleaches and good detergents. For some reason, though, there is a stubborn rule, rumour or misconception out there that insists that you can't wash your embroidery. Why? Provided you have checked that all the dyes are colour-fast – which they should be if you have used good quality thread – you MUST wash your embroidery. It brings it to life.

- Rinse it well in cold water to get rid of any lines that you may have drawn with a washout pen.
- Soak it for a few hours in tepid water mixed with a tablespoon or two of good detergent.
- Swish it around a bit before rinsing it in cold water.
- If you find there are marks – perhaps chalk paper lines – that haven't washed out, scrub them gently with pure soap on a toothbrush.
- Rinse again to make sure that no soap or detergent remains.
- Squeeze out the excess water, place it flat on a towel and roll up the towel.
- Squeeze the towel with the embroidery inside it to get rid of any remaining excess water.
- Stretch the damp embroidery in a hoop or frame that is larger than the embroidered area and place it in front of an open window, out of direct sunlight, to dry in the breeze.
- If you have stretched it well you will probably not need to iron it when it is dry. If you do need to iron it, turn it wrong side up on a folded towel and press the back with an iron set on medium heat.

Materials

FABRICS

Traditional crewel embroidery was done on linen twill fabric. It is still possible to find this fabric but it is hard to come by and expensive when you do track it down. This aside, fabric manufacture has moved on in leaps and bounds since the 17th century. There are so many suitable fabrics out there, that it would be a pity not to take advantage of the vast array that is available.

Choose the fabric that you use for your embroidery with care. It needs to be stable, washable and strong enough to accommodate your stitching. My preference is for fabric that comprises natural fibres like cotton, linen or silk. However, if the project calls for, say, a taffeta then I will quite happily use a synthetic fabric and, likewise, if I come across a fabric that is plain gorgeous, one that is crying out to be used for hand embroidery, I tend to ignore what it is made from.

- Embroidering a project that will be used in your home often requires a heavier fabric than you would use for household linen and framed pictures.
- Projects that will be displayed under glass should be worked on fabric that will be easy to stretch for framing and a lighter fabric is a better choice.
- Assume that fabric is likely to shrink and that any colours may run. Always wash the fabric before transferring the design onto it.

The fabrics used for the projects in this book are described here.

Hopsack

Called hopsack because of its loose construction and similarity to the original flax sacks used to carry hops, this fabric is 100% cotton. This book uses medium hopsack with a weight of 260 gsm. It is heavier than many of the fabrics used for embroidery, and is ideal for soft furnishings and other home embroidery. The natural look of the fabric, sometimes with unbleached seeds still intact, makes it appealing for traditional styles of embroidery.

Dupion silk

The most luxurious of all fabrics, natural silk makes a fine background for embroidery. It does, however, come with some drawbacks. It is coloured with vegetable dyes which are not colour-fast. Consequently, when you are using silk fabric you should wash it in cold water using organic soap. Rinse it until the water is clear. Only then should you trace your design onto the fabric and commence stitching. Another drawback that comes as a result of vegetable dyes is that the fabric may fade. To this end, your finished product should never be displayed in direct sunlight. Silk tears easily and you should be gentle with it when stitching.

TIP

You spend many hours on a project. You should use the best quality materials that you can afford.

Taffeta

A crisp, smooth, plain-woven fabric, taffeta is ideal for embroidery projects that require sheen in the base fabric. It is a particularly appropriate fabric to use in combination with beads and crystals and is available in a wide range of colours. Whilst it is possible to find silk taffeta, most modern taffetas are made with synthetic fibres and come in non-stretch or stretch taffeta.

TIP

If you are using taffeta, take care to choose the non-stretch option for embroidery.

Linen/cotton blend fabric

Projects that will be mounted and framed are best done on a lighter weight fabric than anything that would be used for soft furnishings. I use a good quality linen/cotton blend 200 gsm fabric, which means that when it is stretched prior to picture framing there is not too much bulk to contend with. It washes well, does not lose its shape and has a weave that is close enough for fine stitching. As with all fabrics, I rinse it before I use it, to guard against shrinkage.

Cotton voile

It is advisable to use a backing-fabric for most projects. This provides stability and a place to end off your stitching. Lightweight and smooth, cotton voile in either white or ecru is the perfect fabric to use. It is unlikely to shrink but you should take the precaution of rinsing it in cold water before you use it. Once it is dry and pressed, cut a piece to the same size as the embroidery fabric, tack the two pieces together with horizontal and vertical lines through the middle and machine stitch around the outside edges to prevent fraying.

THREADS AND THEIR NEEDLES

When embroidering, you should endeavour to use quality threads. Their dyes should be colour-fast, they should not break easily and should not develop fluff-balls while you are working with them. The threads used in this book are available worldwide and fulfil the criteria mentioned above.

Stranded cotton

Usually six stranded, this thread comes in skeins of 8 metres. It has a lustrous sheen and you can embroider with as many strands as you wish, depending on the texture you wish to achieve. It is ideal for fine work. This book uses stranded cotton from the DMC and Anchor ranges. Use a size 7 or 10 embroidery needle when stitching with stranded cotton.

Satin thread

Usually six stranded, this man-made fibre makes a shiny thread that is ideal for adding texture and dimension to your work. It is inclined to be lively, but can be tamed by running it through a thread conditioner. This book uses threads from the DMC satin range. Use a size 6 or 7 embroidery needle when stitching with rayon thread.

Perle thread

This twisted thread is available in a variety of sizes and colours, with a sheen that is remarkably effective. It is easy to work with and provides alternative texture to your work. It is ideal for many of the weaving stitches featured and this book uses thread from the DMC and Chameleon ranges of perle threads. Use a size 26 chenille or a size 26 tapestry needle when stitching with perle thread.

Tatting cotton

This book uses DMC Special Dentelles 80 for the needle lace stitches and weaving that is worked in small areas. Similar to perle, it is a twisted thread with a light sheen. Because most needle lace techniques are based on detached buttonhole stitch, the thread tangles easily. To guard against this, run it through a thread conditioner. Use a size 28 or size 26 tapestry needle when stitching with Special Dentelles.

Metallic thread

Although manufactured from 100% polyester yarn, metallic threads have the appearance of metal and are guaranteed to add an exciting dimension to your work, particularly when used in conjunction with beads. These threads shred easily so you should work with short pieces and re-thread often. Thread conditioner provides lubrication and protection, so should be used. This book uses metallic threads from the Madeira Metallic, DMC Light Effects and *Fils Métallisé* ranges. You should use a size 6 or 7 embroidery needle when stitching with metallic threads.

Koeksister thread

Affectionately named for the ladies in Benoni, a small city to the east of Johannesburg, where I first came across the idea, koeksister thread is a chain of thread made on an overlocking machine. Koeksister threads are used in the Inflorescense design and to make your own, refer to the table below. Thread numbers are from the Mettler range of machine embroidery threads.

All machines are slightly different, so when making your thread do some test pieces. Pull the thread as it comes out of the machine. What you are aiming to achieve is a chain of thread that is loose but not loopy. Adjust the settings accordingly. Use a size 20 or 22 chenille needle when stitching with these threads.

BEADS AND CRYSTALS

Beads

When adding beads to your embroidery you should endeavour to seek out the best beads that you can find. Seed beads come from many countries and many different factories. Many of them are badly shaped, of uneven sizing and with holes that are off-centre. The best beads come from Japan and this book uses beads from the Miyuki range of Japanese seed beads.

TIP

Using inferior quality beads ruins the effect of your work.

Bead sizing is determined by the number of beads that fit into an inch which means that, like counted thread linen, the higher the number, the smaller the bead. In this book we use size 15°, size 11° and size 8° round rocailles and #1 (3 mm) bugle beads.

	1 Left Needle	2 Right Needle	3 Left Bottom Thread	4 Right Bottom Thread
Machine Settings	1	¼	1½	2
02 Light Brown	Gold 2108	Cream 870	Dark Tan 853	Light Golden Tan 771
06 Royal Purple	Gold 2108	Purple 3541	Purple 2920	Cream 870
07 Light Green Emerald	Gold 2108	Cream 870	Green 5650	Green 5610

As a general rule, beads are attached to fabric using stranded cotton, the colour of which should be similar to the shade of the bead. It is sometimes better, though, when attaching single beads to use a thread colour that is identical to the background fabric. It can be useful, when working with transparent beads, to attach them with a completely different coloured thread. In this way, you can alter the colour of the bead to create additional shading.

Because the holes in the beads are small and you will need to pass the needle through, sometimes more than once, you have the choice of using a bead embroidery needle, a size 12 quilting needle or a size 11 sharps needle. My preference is for the quilting needles. They are short and bend less. All of these needles have an extremely small eye so you should use only one strand of thread which you then double over for extra strength.

Crystals

To be called crystal, glass must use a minimum of 24% lead or metal oxide in its manufacture. It is the addition of metal that gives the glass a heightened refractive index which is then further exploited by glass-cutters to enhance the sparkle that is typical of crystal. The sizing of crystal rhinestones and beads is metric and indicates either the diameter or the length of the glass object.

Popular with designers of evening wear, I have used Swarovski Flat Back Crystals to enhance two of the designs in this book in an attempt to show hand-embroiderers their value as an addition to Jacobean embroidery.

COPPER WIRE

The use of stumpwork techniques in 'Late Harvest' has necessitated the use of wire for the raised leaves. 24 to 26-gauge wire is suitable for stumpwork and, because I live in a humid part of the world where metal is likely to rust, I use copper wire. Provided you make sure that your stitching covers the wire, it works well and you are unlikely to look at your beautifully embroidered project in a few years' time and find, with horror, that it has rust spots that have eaten through the thread.

Copper wire is not easily bought in hardware shops so I pop down to the industrial area in my town, find a company that does armature winding and beg copper wire off them. I'm always prepared to pay but when I tell them what I want it for they are so non-plussed that they usually give it to me for nothing.

FRAY CHECK

Whether you call it fray-stop, fray-check or no-fray, this liquid has the same purpose: to stop fabric from fraying. The brand you use is unimportant, provided it is a clear liquid that is transparent when it dries. Reject those that are milky in appearance as they distort the colour of the threads when they dry. You will need to apply fray-stop to the edges of the wired leaves in the 'Late Harvest' design before you cut them away from the fabric onto which you have embroidered. No matter how careful you are in its application, it will bleed into the embroidery and that is why it is vital to choose a clear solution.

Tools

The tools required to complete all of the projects in this book appear below.

CUTTING

- Large dressmaking scissors for cutting fabric
- Small, sharp scissors for cutting threads

TRACING

- A light box for transferring designs onto fabric used in conjunction with either a blue tailor's pen, a white washout pen or a soft pencil, or
- Dressmaker's carbon

NEEDLES

- Embroidery/Crewel needles: sizes 7 and 10
- Tapestry needles: sizes 26 and 28
- Chenille needles: sizes 18, 20 or 22
- Quilting needles: sizes 12 or 11; or
- Bead embroidery needle: size 12
- Milliner's or straw needle: size 5
- Long darner needle: size 9

GENERAL TOOLS

- Embroidery hoops – 14", 10" and 7"
- Embroidery frame – Grip n Stitch rectangle frame
- Thread conditioner
- Beading mat or beading tray
- Seam ripper or stitch cutter for unpicking
- Pair of tweezers to get rid of fluff when you are unpicking
- Spinster twisting tool for cord making

STUMPWORK TOOLS

- Small pair of pliers
- Wire cutters

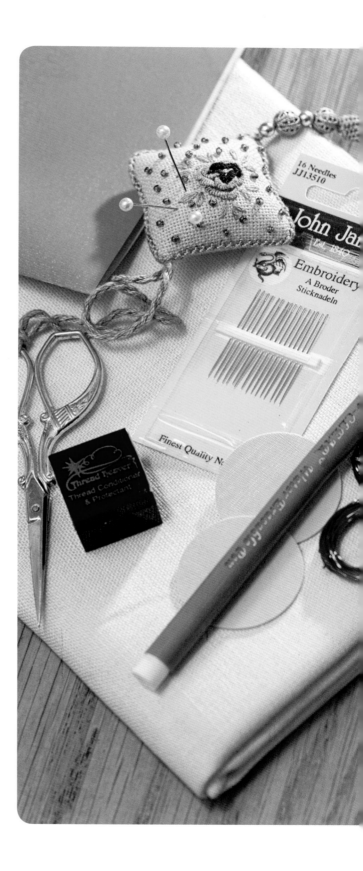

Stitch gallery

The instructions in this gallery provide a general guide for each of the stitches. Number of strands, threads or beads used, variations and other specifics are described in the instructions for each project.

CREWEL STITCHES

Backstitch

Working from right to left, bring the needle up a stitch length before the end of the line you wish to stitch. Go in at the end of the line, coming up again a stitch length away from the beginning of the stitch you are working. Repeat as necessary, keeping your stitch length as even as possible.

Battlement couching

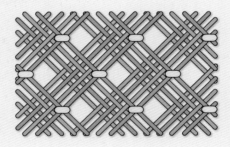

Work a layer of long straight stitches across the area. These can be vertical or diagonal. Work another layer of long straight stitches that are placed at right angles to the first layer (pink layer). Work 3 more layers in different shades of thread (purple, yellow and blue layers). Work small, straight couching stitches over the intersection of the last layer of trellis stitches.

Buttonhole & blanket stitch

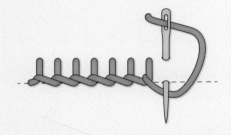

These two stitches are formed in the same way. The difference between the two is that buttonhole stitches are placed close together whilst blanket stitches have gaps between them. Working from left to right, bring the needle up on the bottom edge where you require the ridge. Take the needle in at the top edge, and out again at the bottom edge, with the thread looped under the needle. Pull through and repeat as required. Secure at the end with a small couching stitch over the last one at the ridge edge.

Bullion knot

Come out of the fabric at the start of the space you wish to fill and go in again at the end of that space. Come out again at the start of the space and don't pull the needle all the way through the fabric. Twist the thread around the needle as many times as you require. Holding the twists with the thumb and fore-finger of your left hand, pull the needle through. Pull the working thread until the knot lies flat and take the needle back into the fabric at the start of the space.

Chain stitch

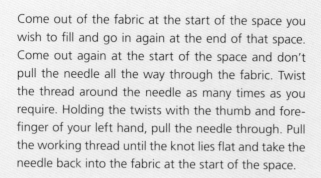

Bring the needle up on the line and pull through. Take the needle back into the same hole, loop the thread under the needle and pull through. Staying inside the loop, go back into the same hole, loop the thread under the needle and pull through. Repeat as required and catch the last loop with a small couching stitch.

Coral stitch

Working from left to right, bring your needle up at the beginning of the line. Make a small stitch under the line, take the working thread over and then under the needle. Pull through, first backwards and then forwards, to tighten the small knot.

Couching

Use two threaded needles. Bring the first one up at the beginning of the line and lay it down. Catch it down with small stitches placed at intervals along the line. These stitches should not have a tight tension.

Detached buttonhole stitch

Surround the area that you intend to fill with small backstitches which will be what you use to anchor the detached buttonhole stitch. Bring your needle up on the side, as indicated in the diagram, go over and under the first horizontal backstitch and making sure that the working thread is under the needle, pull through to form a buttonhole stitch. Snake through the vertical backstitches at the end of the row. The second and subsequent rows are anchored in the loops between the stitches.

Detached chain (Lazy Daisy)

Bring the needle up on the line and pull through. Take the needle back into the same hole, loop the thread under the needle and pull through. Catch the loop with a small couching stitch.

Drizzle stitch

Bring the threaded needle up through the fabric, remove the thread from the eye of the needle. Put the needle back into the fabric just next to where you came up. Place the thread over your left index finger and rotate your finger to form a loop. Transfer that loop onto the needle, pull the working thread so that it goes down to the base. This is a cast-on stitch. Cast on as many stitches as you need. Without removing it from the fabric, rethread the needle and pull the thread down through the cast-on stitches to the back of the fabric.

Fly stitch

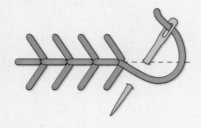

Start at the tip of your shape with a straight stitch. Come up on the left of that stitch, go in at the same level on the right, leaving a loop. Come up in the bottom hole of the straight stitch. Catch the loop and pull through. Make a straight stitch.

French knot

Bring the needle up through the fabric, twist the thread over the needle once or twice and tighten. Go back into the fabric just next to where you came out. Pull the twists that are around the needle down to the bottom. Hold the thread and pull the needle through to form the knot.

Heavy chain stitch

Make a small backstitch at the beginning of the line. Bring the needle up below the backstitch, go under the backstitch and back into where you came out to create a loop. Bring the needle up below the loop you have just made and make another loop through the backstitch. Bring the needle up below the loop you have just made and make a loop through the first loop. Continue by bringing the needle up below the loop just done and making a loop through the second last loop you made.

Knotted pearl stitch

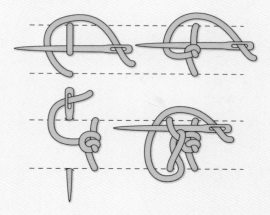

Bring your needle through the fabric halfway between the two lines. Take it down directly above that on the top line. Come up on the bottom line. Take it under the stitch at the top, pulling through with the free thread under the needle to form a small, intertwined knot. Take the needle under that same stitch, again pulling through with the free thread under the needle to form a second knot. Take the needle through the fabric on the top line to form a diagonal straight stitch. Come up on the bottom line. Take it under the diagonal straight stitch at the top, pulling through with the free thread under the needle to form a small, intertwined knot. Take the needle under that same stitch, again pulling through with the free thread under the needle to form a second knot. Take the needle through the fabric on the top line to form a diagonal straight stitch. Come up on the bottom line. Continue in this way, finishing off by going into the fabric once you have completed the second knot in the last stitch sequence.

Long & short stitch

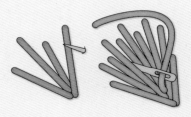

Work with 1 strand of thread. Starting in the middle of the shape working first to the right and then returning to the middle and working to the left, stitch the darkest colour at the base first. Work straight stitches of random lengths from top to bottom fanning the stitches so that they favour the centre. Change to the medium colour thread for the next row, which is started slightly above the darkest colour. Work the stitches going into the fabric between the threads in the previous row. These stitches should also be of random lengths, making them alternately long and short on both ends. Change to the lightest colour for the top row. Following the top outline of the shape, work the third row going into the fabric between the threads in the previous row. These stitches should also be of random lengths, with the ragged edge at the bottom of the row.

Overcasting stitch

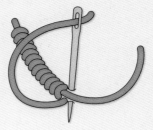

Couch foundation threads, or stumpwork wire, into place. Starting at the beginning of the line, bring the needle up on one side of the foundation threads and take it back into the fabric on the other side of the foundation threads. Come up again at the start of the previous stitch.

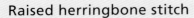

Raised herringbone stitch

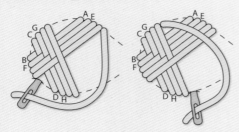

Bring your needle up at A. Take it back in again at B. Come up at C and go down at D. Bring it up again at E and go into the fabric at F. Keep going in this way until your shape has been filled. A subtle ridge will form in the centre of the shape.

Raised stem stitch

Working from right to left, create a straight stitch ladder which forms the basis of this technique. Working from left to right bring your needle up slightly past the last straight stitch in the ladder. Go over and under the straight stitches in continuous lines.

Romanian stitch

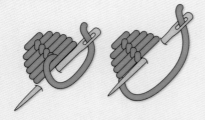

Bring your needle up on the left outline of the shape. Go back down on the right outline and come up on the centre line and pull the thread through so that the long stitch falls below the needle. Do a small couching stitch over the long stitch.

Satin stitch

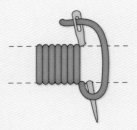

Working from left to right, bring your needle up at the bottom and in at the top, and come out at the bottom again. Place your stitches close together so that no fabric is showing. It is best to work over the shortest side and stitches can also be placed diagonally.

Split stitch

It is usually best to do this stitch with 2 strands of thread. Come up at the beginning of the line. Go in again a little way along and before pulling through, come up again in the middle of the stitch, taking your needle up between the 2 strands of thread. Pull through to tighten.

Stem stitch

Working from left to right, come up just above the line, go in just below the line and come up halfway back, just above the line. Pull through. When using stem stitch as an outline stitch, come up on the line and go in on the line.

Straight stitch

Bring your needle up at the beginning of the stitch and take it into the fabric at the end of the stitch. Stitches can be of equal or unequal length, or as directed in the instructions in your embroidery pattern.

Trellis couching – basic

Work a layer of long straight stitches across the area. These can be vertical or diagonal. Work another layer of long straight stitches that are placed at right angles to the first layer. Work small, straight couching stitches over the intersection of the stitches.

Trellis couching – cross stitch filling

Using thread shade 1 (pink lines), work a layer of pairs of long straight stitches across the area. These can be horizontal or diagonal. Work another layer (orange lines) of pairs of long straight stitches that are placed at right angles to the first layer. Using thread shade 2 (yellow lines), work small, straight couching stitches over each thread of the intersections. Work from the outside into the middle of each intersection, each stitch going into the same hole.

Trellis couching – woven

Using thread shade 1 (green lines), work a layer of long straight stitches across the area. These can be horizontal or diagonal. Work another layer of long straight stitches that are placed at right angles to the first layer. Using thread shade 2 (yellow lines), work small, straight couching stitches over the intersection of the stitches. Using thread shade 3 (blue lines), weave over and under the shade 1 lines. Using thread shade 4 and working at right angles (jade lines), weave under the first layer of trellis (green lines) and over the weaving that you have just done (blue lines).

Vermicelli couching

Thread a needle with 2 strands of thread and another with 1 strand of thread. Come through the fabric with the 2-strand needle and couch that thread into a series of rounded squiggles that move all over the area that you wish to cover, but never cross over each other. At the edges of the section go into the fabric and come up again further along continuing the pattern.

Whipped backstitch

To whip backstitch, bring your needle up adjacent to the beginning of the line of stitching. Take your needle and thread over, then under each stitch. It is advisable to use a tapestry needle when whipping. A contrasting colour thread is often effective.

Whipped spider's web filling

Working from left to right, create a straight stitch ladder which forms the basis of this technique. Working from right to left bring your needle up slightly past the last straight stitch in the ladder. Go under the first stitch. Go back over and under the same stitch and under the next straight stitch. Do continuous lines.

Whipped stem stitch

To whip stem stitch, bring your needle up adjacent to the beginning of the line of stem stitch. Take your needle and thread over, then under the section where that stitch and the next stitch lie adjacent to one another. It is advisable to use a tapestry needle when whipping. A contrasting colour thread is often effective.

COMBINATION STITCHES

Chain and backstitch combination

Work a row of chain stitch using shade 1. Thereafter, using shade 2, work backstitches from the middle of the first chain stitch to the space just before the start of the chain stitch. Follow that with backstitches that start in the middle of the next chain stitch and go into the start of the backstitch in the previous chain stitch. Continue doing backstitch in this way, finishing up on the outside of the last chain stitch. When you do multiple rows of this stitch combination, it is sensible to complete the backstitch in the row before moving onto the next row of chain stitch because it is difficult to see where you should stitch if you have done all of the chain stitch before you start on the backstitch.

BEAD EMBROIDERY STITCHES

Bead-couching

Pick up not less than 2 and not more than 5 beads. Lay them along the line that you need to follow, estimate about the width of a bead and go through the fabric. Push the beads to the beginning and couch over the thread between each bead, pulling the line into place as you go. Bring the needle up immediately after the last bead and pick up the next group of beads. Keep going in this way. When you reach the end of the line, go through the fabric, catch the thread in the voile backing fabric and return through the same hole. Run the thread through the whole line of beads, going into the fabric at the beginning and tugging the thread to tighten. This pulls the line of beads neatly into place.

Beaded palestrina stitch

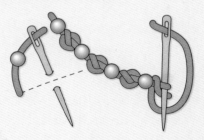

Working from left to right, come up at the beginning of the line. Pick up a bead and leaving sufficient space for the bead, go into the fabric on top of the line, coming out below the line. Pull through. Go over and under the thread. Go over and under the thread again in the space between where you went in and came up through the fabric. Make sure the loop of thread is under the needle. Pull through and tighten the knot that forms. Repeat as required. End on a knot and take your thread to the back to end off.

Beaded fly stitch

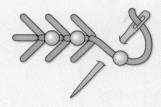

Start at the tip with a 4 mm straight stitch. Come up on the left and go down on the right of the straight stitch, leaving a loop. Come up at the bottom of the straight stitch, catching the loop before you tighten. Pick up a bead and go into the fabric below it, leaving enough room for the bead to sit happily. Leaving a space of about 1 mm on the left side, start the next fly stitch.

Covering a large bead with thread

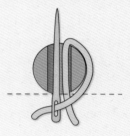

Bring your needle up through the fabric slightly off the centre of the area in which you want to place the bead, picking up the bead at the same time. Holding the bead in place with your finger, take the thread over the bead, going back into the fabric at the side of the bead. Take the needle through at an angle so that it pierces the fabric slightly below the bead. Do four stitches that divide the area that you have to cover into quarters. Thereafter fill in those quarters with the same kind of stitches. Try to place them systematically so that the thread cover is neat and keep going until the hole in the middle of the large bead is almost full. On the last stitch, come up through the middle, pick up a small bead, go down through the middle of the large bead pulling tight so that the small bead sits in the dent in the middle of the large bead.

STITCHES BASED ON NEEDLE LACE TECHNIQUES

Needle lace stitch no. 4

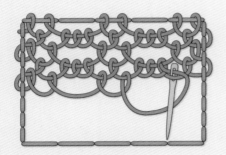

- Outline the shape with backstitch.
- Choose the longest, smoothest side of the shape for the first row.
- Come up at the side, approximately level with where the ridge of the detached buttonhole will lie.
- [Working from left to right, do a group of two detached buttonhole stitches in each alternate backstitch along the top.]
- Repeat from [to] until you get to the end of the row.
- Go through the nearest backstitch level with the ridge of the detached buttonhole in the row you have just done.
- Snake down through the next backstitch.
- # [Working from right to left, do a detached buttonhole stitch into the gap between the pair of detached buttonhole stitches in the previous row.
- Do three detached buttonhole stitches in the longer gap leading up to the next pair of detached buttonhole stitches in the previous row.]
- Repeat from [to] until you reach the end of the row.
- Snake down to start the next row.
- Do a single detached buttonhole stitch on either side of the single detached buttonhole stitches in the previous row. When you reach the end of the row snake down to start the next row.#
- Continue the pattern by repeating the last two rows from # to #.
- When you have filled the space, attach the last row to the backstitch at the bottom by going through the loop and the backstitch immediately below it

as you form each detached buttonhole. Whip the backstitches in between to bury the loop. (Refer to the section Last Row which appears at the end of the needle lace Stitch Gallery).

Needle lace stitch no. 7

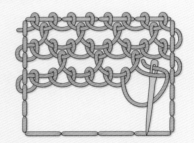

1. Outline the shape with backstitch.

2. Choose the longest, smoothest side of the shape for the first row. Come up at the side, approximately level with where the ridge of the detached buttonhole will lie.

3. [Working from left to right, do a group of two detached buttonhole stitches into each backstitch along the top.] Repeat from [to] until you get to the end of the row.

4. Go through the nearest backstitch level with the ridge of the detached buttonhole in the row you have just done. Snake down through the next backstitch.

5. Working from right to left, do a detached buttonhole stitch into the gap between the last two detached buttonhole stitches in the previous row.

6. [Miss a gap and do a single detached buttonhole stitch into the next gap.] Repeat from [to] until you reach the end of the row.

7. Snake down to start the next row.

8. #Do two detached buttonhole stitches into the large loops between the detached buttonhole stitches in the previous row. When you reach the end of the row, snake down to start the next row.

9. Do a detached buttonhole stitch in each of the gaps between the two detached buttonhole stitches in the previous row. When you reach the end of the row, snake down to start the next row.#

10. Continue the pattern by repeating the last two rows from # to #.

11. When you have filled the space, attach the last row to the backstitch at the bottom by going through the loop and the backstitch immediately below it as you form each detached buttonhole. Whip the backstitches in between to bury the loop. (Refer to the section Last Row which appears at the end of the needle lace Stitch Gallery).

Needle lace stitch no. 8

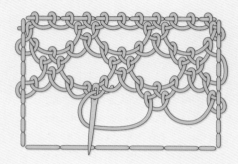

1. Outline the shape with backstitch.

2. Choose the longest side of the shape for the first row. Come up at the side, approximately level with where the ridge of the detached buttonhole will lie.

3. Working from left to right, do a group of two detached buttonhole stitches in every backstitch along the top.

4. Go through the nearest backstitch level with the ridge of the detached buttonhole in the row you have just done. Snake down through the next backstitch.

5. Working from right to left, do a detached buttonhole stitch into the gap before the last detached buttonhole stitch in the previous row.

6. Do a detached buttonhole stitch into the gap between the next two stitches in the previous row.

7. [Miss two gaps and do a single detached buttonhole stitch into each of the next two gaps.]

8. Repeat from [to] until you reach the end of the row. Snake down to start the next row.

9. #Do three detached buttonhole stitches into the large loops and one detached buttonhole stitch in the gap between the pairs of detached buttonhole

stitches in the previous row. When you reach the end of the row, snake down to start the next row.

10. Do a detached buttonhole stitch in each of the two middle gaps between the three detached buttonhole stitches in the large loop in the previous row. When you reach the end of the row, snake down to start the next row.#

11. Continue the pattern by repeating the last two rows from # to #.

12. Attach the last row to the backstitch at the bottom by going through the loop and the backstitch immediately below it as you form each detached buttonhole. Whip the backstitches in between to bury the loop. (Refer to the section Last Row which appears at the end of the needle lace Stitch Gallery).

Needle lace stitch no. 9

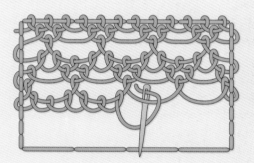

1. Outline the shape with backstitch.

2. Choose the longest, smoothest side of the shape for the first row. Come up at the side, approximately level with where the ridge of the detached buttonhole will lie.

3. Working from left to right, do a group of two detached buttonhole stitches in every backstitch along the top.

4. Go through the nearest backstitch level with the ridge of the detached buttonhole in the row you have just done. Snake down through the next backstitch.

5. Working back in the direction from which you have come, miss the first gap between the last two buttonholes that you did in the previous row.

6. *#Do a detached buttonhole in each of the following two gaps. Miss the next gap.#

7. Repeat from # to # until you get to the other side.

8. Go through the nearest backstitch level with the ridge of the detached buttonhole in the row you have just done. Snake down through the next backstitch.

9. Working back in the direction from which you have come, #do a detached buttonhole stitch between each pair of stitches that you did in the previous row.#

10. Repeat from # to # until you get to the other side.

11. Go through the nearest backstitch level with the ridge of the detached buttonhole in the row you have just done. Snake down through the next backstitch.

12. Working back in the direction from which you have come, do 3 detached buttonhole stitches into each of the large loops that formed between the stitches in the previous row.

13. When you get to the other side, go through the nearest backstitch level with the ridge of the detached buttonhole in the row you have just done. Snake down through the next backstitch.*

14. Continue the pattern by repeating the last three rows from * to *.

15. When you have filled the space, attach the last row to the backstitch at the bottom by going through the loop and the backstitch immediately below it as you form each detached buttonhole. Whip the back-stitches in between to bury the loop. (Refer to the section Last Row which appears at the end of the needle lace Stitch Gallery).

Needle lace stitch no. 23

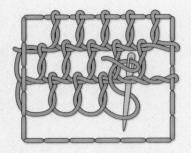

1. Outline the shape with backstitch.

2. Choose the longest, smoothest side of the shape for the first row.

3. Come up at the side, approximately level with where the ridge of the first row of stitches will lie.

4. Go over and under the first backstitch at the top, twist the working thread over and under the needle and pull through to form a detached buttonhole-type stitch, with a twist in the bar. This is known as a tulle bar.

5. The first row consists of a tulle bar in each backstitch.

6. *Go through the nearest backstitch level with the ridge of the tulle bar in the row you have just done.

7. Return to the beginning of the row by whipping the thread that forms every gap between the tulle bars. Snake down through the next backstitch.*

8. [For the next row, work a tulle bar into every gap between the tulle bars in the previous row.

9. Repeat from * to *.]

10. Repeat from [to] until you have filled the space. Try to space the rows in such a way that you are able to attach the needle lace to the backstitch at the bottom on the return row, whipping through the gaps and the backstitch at the same time.

Needle lace stitch no. 26

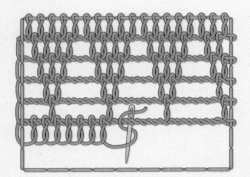

1. Outline the shape with backstitch.

2. Choose the longest, smoothest side of the shape for the first row.

3. Come up at the side, approximately level with where the ridge of the first row of stitches will lie.

4. Go over and under the first backstitch at the top, twist the working thread over and under the needle and pull through to form a detached buttonhole-type stitch, with a twist in the bar. This is known as a tulle bar.

5. The first row consists of a tulle bar in each backstitch.

6. *Go through the nearest backstitch level with the ridge of the tulle bar in the row you have just done.

7. Return to the beginning of the row by whipping the thread that forms every gap between the tulle bars.

8. Snake down through the next backstitch.*

9. Miss the first gap. [Work tulle bars into the next four gaps, miss a gap.] Repeat from [to] until you reach the other side.

10. Repeat from * to * whipping the larger gap between the groups of 4 tulle bars twice.

11. Now do a row with sets of 3 tulle bars placed in the small gaps between the 4 bars in the row above.

12. Repeat from * to * whipping the larger gap between the groups of 3 tulle bars three times.

13. Continue in this way, doing sets of 2 tulle bars, followed by a row with 1 tulle bar. Every time you return, add an extra whipping stitch in the large gap between the tulle bars.

14. Start the pattern again by working 5 tulle bars into the large gap between the single bars that you did at the end of the last pattern sequence.

15. Try to space the rows in such a way that you are able to attach the needle lace to the backstitch at the bottom on the return row, whipping through the gaps and the backstitch at the same time.

Needle lace picot

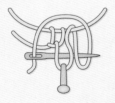

Take the needle over and under the loop onto which the preceding detached buttonhole stitches have been attached, catching the thread under a pin, which you have placed slightly below the point where the ridge of the detached buttonhole stitch lies. Turning your work to the right, so that you will be pulling towards yourself, work a detached buttonhole stitch over the threads that are held by the pin, as indicated in the

diagram, and making sure that the needle goes over the free thread to form a buttonhole stitch. Turning your work left again, to face the way you were working, continue straight into the next, ordinary, detached buttonhole stitch that will be formed, as usual, over the loop. Note that a picot can be made with additional detached buttonhole stitches over the threads that are held by the pin, in which case you work those before continuing with the normal stitches that are formed over the loop at the top.

Needle lace – last row

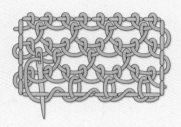

All needle lace techniques based on detached buttonhole stitch should be finished off in the same way, unless the last row has been described in the stitch instructions.

1. Continue working the detached buttonhole stitches until you reach the bottom of the section that you intend to fill. It does not matter whether you are working a right to left, or a left to right row. For the purposes of these instructions we are going to assume you have worked a left to right row to correspond with the diagram on the left.

2. At the end of the row, instead of snaking through the backstitch, take the needle through the fabric to the other side.

3. Bring the needle up directly below the backstitch at the bottom, just in from the corner on the right.

4. The last row continues the pattern of the technique and attaches the needle lace to the backstitch at the same time.

5. Depending on how far you need to travel to make the first buttonhole stitch in the pattern you may need to whip the first backstitch so that the loop, which would otherwise form, becomes lost. In the diagram above this has not been necessary.

6. Working from right to left, form the detached buttonhole stitch which goes through the loop by taking the needle through the loop in the previous row and through the backstitch at the same time. Make sure that the working thread is below the tip of the needle.

7. Pull the needle through to form the detached buttonhole stitch, making sure that the lace pulls down and stretches over the shape that you have covered.

8. Whip the next backstitch to lose the loop and create the next detached buttonhole stitch.

9. Continue in this way until you reach the left corner. The needle lace should be attached and evenly stretched over the entire section.

10. Take your needle through the fabric to end off at the back.

NEEDLE WEAVING

How to read these stitch instructions:

- Work the warp stitches first using a size 7 embroidery needle. These are long, straight stitches that go from the top edge of the shape to the bottom edge directly below, following the lines that demarcate the edge.
- Referring to 'Warp' at the beginning of each stitch, determine the colour of the thread, whether there is more than one colour and, if so, how many warp stitches are to be worked in each of the colours.
- Once your warp stitches are in place, move on to 'Weft'. Determine the colour or colours of thread that you will need to use and thread each colour separately on a size 24 or 26 tapestry needle.
- Take note of the number of rows in each pattern repeat. These are the numbered rows and when you have worked all of them, return to the first row working as many pattern repeats as you need to fill the shape that you have.
- 'O' means go over and 'U' means go under one or more warp threads.
- If the beginning of the row has instructions in brackets, you only work these stitches at the beginning. When you reach the end of the instructions for that row, return to and work from the instruction immediately after the closing bracket.

Single Weaving

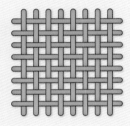

Warp: colour 1
Weft: colour 1 or 2 (pattern repeat 2 rows)

1. O1, U1
2. (U1) O1, U1

Double Weaving

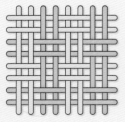

Warp: colour 1
Weft: colour 1 or 2 (pattern repeat 4 rows)

1. (U2) O2, U2
2. (U2) O2, U2
3. O2, U2
4. O2, U2

Texture No. 1

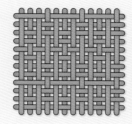

Warp: colour 1
Weft: colour 1 (pattern repeat 8 rows)

1. (U1) O3, U1
2. O1, U3
3. O1, U1
4. (U2) O1, U3
5. (U1) O1, U1
6. (U2) O1, U3
7. O1, U3
8. O1, U1

Texture No. 2

Warp: colour 1
Weft: colour 2 (pattern repeat 8 rows)

1. O1, U1
2. *(U1) O3, U1*
3. Repeat * to *
4. Repeat * to *
5. O1, U1
6. #(O2, U1) O3, U1#
7. Repeat # to #
8. Repeat # to #

Texture No. 4

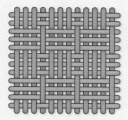

Warp: colour 1
Weft: colour 2 (pattern repeat 11 rows)

1. *O1, U3*
2. Repeat * to *
3. #(U1) O3, U1#
4. Repeat # to #
5. Repeat # to #
6. Repeat * to *
7. Repeat * to *
8. Repeat * to *
9. Repeat # to #
10. Repeat # to #
11. Repeat # to #

Texture No. 7

Warp: colour 1
Weft: colour 2 (pattern repeat 6 rows)

1. (U2) O2, U2
2. (U2) O2, U2
3. (U1) O1, U3
4. O2, U2
5. O2, U2
6. O1, U3

Texture No. 9

Warp: colour 1
Weft: colour 1 or 2 (pattern repeat 6 rows)

1. (U3) O1, U3
2. (U3) O1, U3
3. (U3) O1, U3
4. O3, U1
5. O3, U1
6. O3, U1

Check & Stripes No. 2

Warp: 4 x colour 1; 4 x colour 2
Weft: 4 x colour 1; 4 x colour 2 (pattern repeat 8 rows)

Colour 2:
1. O1, U2
2. (U2) O1, U2
3. (U1) O1, U2
4. O1, U2

Colour 1:
5. (U2) O1, U2
6. (U1) O1, U2
7. O1, U2
8. U2, O1

Check & Stripes No. 4

Warp: 4 x colour 1; 4 x colour 2
Weft: 2 x colour 1; 2 x colour 2 (pattern repeat 4 rows)

Colour 1
1. (U2) O1, U2
2. O1, U2

Colour 2
3. (U2) O1, U2
4. (U1) O1, U2

Check & Stripes No. 5

Warp: 10 x colour 1; 2 x colour 2
Weft: 5 x colour 2; 3 x colour 1 (pattern repeat 8 rows)

Colour 1:
1. (U1) O1, U2
2. O1, U2
3. (U1) O1, U2

Colour 2
4. (U2) O1, U2
5. O1, U1
6. (U1) O1, U1
7. O1, U1
8. (U2) O1, U2

Check & Stripes No. 6

Warp: colour 1
Weft: colour 1; colour 2 (pattern repeat 10 rows)

Colour 1
1. O1, U1
2. U1, O1

Colour 2
3. O3, U1
4. (O1, U1) O3, U1
5. O3, U1

Colour 1
6. U1, O1
7. O1, U1

Colour 2
8. (U1) O3, U1
9. (O2, U1) O3, U1
10. (U1) O3, U1

Check & Stripes No. 7

Warp: 6 x colour 1; 6 x colour 2
Weft: 6 x colour 1; 6 x colour 2 (pattern repeat 12 rows)

Colour 1
1. O2, U2
2. O2, U2
3. (U2) O2, U2
4. (U2) O2, U2
5. O2, U2
6. O2, U2

Colour 2
7. (U2) O2, U2
8. (U2) O2, U2
9. O2, U2
10. O2, U2
11. (U2) O2, U2
12. (U2) O2, U2

Check & Stripes No. 8

Warp: 4 x colour 1; 4 x colour 2
Weft: 4 x colour 1; 4 x colour 2 (pattern repeat 8 rows)

Colour 1
1. (U2) O2, U2
2. (U2) O2, U2
3. O2, U2
4. O2, U2

Colour 2
5. (U2) O2, U2
6. (U2) O2, U2
7. O2, U2
8. O2, U2

Check & Stripes No. 9

Warp: 6 x colour 1; 6 x colour 2
Weft: 2 x colour 1; 2 x colour 2 (pattern repeat 4 rows)

Colour 1
1. (U2) O2, U2
2. (U2) O2, U2

Colour 2
3. O2, U2
4. O2, U2

Check & Stripes No. 10
(pattern repeat 8 rows)

Warp:
1. 2 x colour 1
2. #2 x colour 2
3. 2 x colour 3
4. 2 x colour 1
5. 2 x colour 4
6. 2 x colour 1

7. 2 x colour 3
8. 2 x colour 2
9. 2 x colour 1#
10. Repeat # to #

Weft:

1. 2 x colour 1: (U2) O2, U2 for two rows
2. 2 x colour 2: ** O2, U2 for two rows
3. 2 x colour 3: (U2) O2, U2 for two rows
4. 2 x colour 1: O2, U2 for two rows
5. 2 x colour 4: (U2) O2, U2 for two rows
6. 2 x colour 1: O2, U2 for two rows
7. 2 x colour 3: (U2) O2, U2 for two rows
8. 2 x colour 2: O2, U2 for two rows
9. 2 x colour 1: (U2) O2, U2 for two rows**
10. Repeat ** to **

Check & Stripes No. 11
(pattern repeat 17 rows)

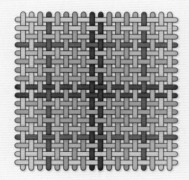

Warp:

1. 2 x colour 1
2. #1 x colour 2
3. 1 x colour 3
4. 1 x colour 1
5. 3 x colour 4
6. 2 x colour 5
7. 3 x colour 4
8. 1 x colour 2
9. 1 x colour 3
10. 1 x colour 1#
11. Repeat # to #

Weft:

1. Colour 1: O1, U1
2. **Colour 1: (U1) O1, U1
3. Colour 2: O1, U1
4. Colour 3: (U1) O1, U1
5. Colour 2: O1, U1
6. Colour 4: (U1) O1, U1
7. Colour 4: O1, U1
8. Colour 4: (U1) O1, U1
9. Colour 5: O1, U1
10. Colour 5: (U1) O1, U1
11. Colour 4: O1, U1
12. Colour 4: (U1) O1, U1
13. Colour 4: O1, U1
14. Colour 2: (U1) O1, U1
15. Colour 3: O1, U1
16. Colour 2: (U1) O1, U1
17. Colour 1: O1, U1**
18. Repeat **to **

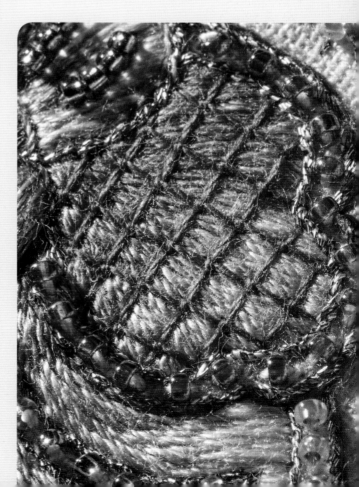

TWISTED STITCHES

The easiest way to convert stranded cotton into a cord with which to embroider is to acquire a Spinster twisting tool. It is however possible to twist it by turning it between your index finger and thumb, or to place a pencil in the loop and turn that.

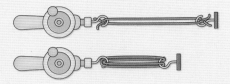

1. Cut a 2-strand length of thread that measures approximately 1 metre (1 yard).
2. Tie an overhand knot on each end of the thread.
3. Loop one end over something that won't move, like a cup-hook or a door knob.
4. Loop the other end over the hook on the Spinster and pull the yarn taut.
5. Now wind the threads until they are firmly twisted together. Test from time to time by relaxing the tension and allowing the threads to twist around one another.
6. When you are happy with the twist, double the twisted thread over by placing the two ends together.
7. Hang the Spinster, or something heavy, at the fold to add weight so that it will twist together evenly.
8. Pull all the threads off the cup-hook (or door knob).
9. Holding the ends together, allow the thread to hang from your fingers and twist freely.
10. Once they stop twisting, do an overhand knot at the raw ends to keep them together. Snip off the raw ends after the knot for the sake of neatness.
11. Thread the folded end onto a size 22 or 24 chenille needle and embroider with it as if it were normal thread.

Twisted couching

When couching with twisted thread, use a size 22 or 24 chenille needle for the twisted thread. Thread a separate needle with one strand of the same thread. Bring the twisted thread up at the beginning of the line, or outline, as you would with normal couching described in the crewel stitches section at the beginning of this gallery. Couch with the single thread. You should not, however, take your couching thread over the whole cord. Catch only the lower twist with the single strand. Try to make this stitch invisible.

A sherry for Jack

RECTANGULAR JACOBEAN PANEL

Dimensions: 225 mm (8⁵⁵⁄₆₄") wide by 105 mm (4⁹⁄₆₄") high

The original of this design has been mounted in a walnut tray. It can be purchased online and website details appear in the Buyer's Guide at the back of this book. It can, however, be framed or used as a cushion panel. The line drawing for this design can be found at the back of the book and should be photocopied to size.

Materials

FABRIC

300 x 430 mm (12 x 17") winter white dupion silk
300 x 430 mm (12 x 17") cotton voile backing fabric

NEEDLES

Size 7 Embroidery Needles
Size 26 Tapestry Needles
Size 10 Embroidery Needles
Size 10 Bead Embroidery Needles

THREAD & BEADS

DMC STRANDED COTTON

Ecru	Ecru
0154	Very Dark Grape
0738	Very Light Tan
0739	Ultra Very Light Tan
0924	Very Dark Grey Green
0926	Medium Grey Green
0927	Light Grey Green
0928	Very Light Grey Green
3011	Dark Khaki Green
3012	Medium Khaki Green
3013	Light Khaki Green
3051	Dark Green Grey
3052	Medium Green Grey
3053	Light Green Grey
3685	Very Dark Mauve
3687	Mauve
3688	Medium Mauve
3689	Light Mauve
3781	Dark Mocha Brown
3790	Ultra Dark Beige Grey
3803	Dark Mauve
3834	Dark Grape
3835	Medium Grape
3836	Light Grape

DMC SPECIAL DENTELLES

Ecru	Ecru
0369	Very Light Pistachio Green
0397*	Light Grape
0738	Very Light Tan
3052*	Medium Green Grey
3688	Medium Mauve

DMC FILS MÉTALLISÉ

4018	Metallic Bright Pink
4052	Metallic Bright Green
4270	Metallic Purple Black

MADEIRA METALLIC: ART. 9842 NO. 40

425	Bronze Black
442	Steel Black

MIYUKI BEADS

8°645	2g	Dyed Dark Rose Silver Lined Alabaster
11°313	2g	Cranberry Gold Luster
15°196	2g	24 carat Yellow Gold Lined Opal
15°313	2g	Cranberry Gold Luster
15°459	2g	Metallic Olive
15°1650	2g	Dyed Semi-Matte Silver Lined Lavender

*These threads were discontinued during the designing of this book. Refer to the Conversion Charts on page 150 for alternative threads.

STITCH INSTRUCTIONS

- Use one strand of thread, unless otherwise stated.
- The design has been divided into sections. Each section is described in detail.

Flower 1 (far right)

TIP

To prevent snarling and twisting run both special dentelles and perle threads through a thread conditioner before you thread them onto a needle.

5. Fill the two darker areas that lie on each side of the needle weaving with padded buttonhole stitch.
6. Using 2 strands of 3685 on a size 7 embroidery needle, pad each area with stem stitch worked from top to bottom.
7. Using 1 strand of the same thread on a size 10 embroidery needle and working at right angles to the padding, cover it with closely worked buttonhole stitch.

TIP

When working with metallic thread use a bigger needle than you might otherwise have chosen. This opens up a channel for the thread and helps to prevent shredding.

1. Referring to the needle weaving stitches in the Stitch Gallery, fill the centre of this flower with the stitch referred to as check and stripes no. 2.
2. Use Special Dentelles 3688 for shade 1 and Special Dentelles Ecru for shade 2.
3. Use a size 7 embroidery needle to work the warp threads and a size 26 tapestry needle for the weft threads.
4. When you have completed the padded buttonhole stitch that is on the left and right of the needle weaving, couch a line of *Fils Métallisé* 4018 in the ditches that lie between the sections.

8. Referring to the needle weaving stitches in the Stitch Gallery fill the centre of this flower with the stitch referred to as texture no. 2.

9. Use Special Dentelles 369 for the warp threads and Special Dentelles 3052 for the weft.

10. Use a size 7 embroidery needle to work the warp threads and a size 26 tapestry needle for the weft threads.

11. Using a size 10 embroidery needle, pad the outer edge of each leaf with stem stitch using 2 strands of 3053.

12. Do satin stitch over the padding using 1 strand of the same thread on the same size needle.

13. Start with a vertical stitch that comes out at the tip of the leaf and goes in at the tip of the needle weaving. From there, slowly fan the stitches until you have reached a diagonal direction, at which point you stop fanning further and keep your stitches at that angle.

14. Using 1 strand of 3051 threaded onto a size 10 embroidery needle stitch a line of backstitch in the ditch between the weaving and the satin stitch.

15. Whip the backstitch with *Fils Métallisé* 4052.

16. Outline the outer edges of the padded satin stitch with stem stitch using 1 strand of 3051.

17. Fill the middle section of each of these petals with long and short stitch shading.

18. Starting at the base with 739, shade up to Ecru on the tip. Use a size 10 embroidery needle.

19. Fill the outer section of each petal with 3 rows of chain and backstitch combination – see the combination stitches section in the Stitch Gallery.

20. Use 3685 for the first chain stitch row, followed by 3803 for the middle row and 3687 for the outer row.

21. Use *Fils Métallisé* 4018 for the backstitch.

22. Outline the outer edge of each petal with a fine stem stitch using 3685.

23. Using 3051 fill each of the leaves with raised herringbone stitch.

24. Outline each leaf with fine stem stitch using the same thread.

25. Using a strand of 3658 threaded onto a size 10 embroidery needle, come up in the middle of the circle.

26. Pick up a size 8°645 and a size 15°313 bead. Return through the large bead leaving the smaller bead to hold it in place.

27. Bring your needle up adjacent to the large bead.

28. Pick up 9 x size 11°313 beads.

29. Take the needle back through the first 3 beads to form a circle.

30. Tighten the thread, manipulating it so that the circle of beads lies around the larger bead in the middle.

31. Go down, through the fabric and thereafter come up between each bead and couch over the thread that is holding them. Take care to manipulate the beads into a neat circle as you go along.

Flower 2 (five-petal checked)

Each of the coloured blocks in the five petals of this flower is filled with padded satin stitch. Thread an arm's length single strand of 924 onto a size 10 embroidery needle. Double it over and secure with a knot. Work horizontal satin stitch padding over the width of the block. Secure at the back with a knot and snip one of the strands. This will leave you with a single strand of thread. Now use this single strand of thread to do vertical satin stitch over the padding. Change the direction of the padded satin stitch every time you move to the next block, placing the stitches at right angles to the previous block. When moving to the next row, ensure that the direction of the stitching in each block is placed at right angles to the row above.

Three of the petals have four horizontal rows of blocks. Starting from the top row, working from left to right the threads you should use are as listed in the table below:

3836	738	3685	Ecru
3013	3687	926	3790
928	3834	3012	3689
3687	3013	Ecru	3835

1. Using two strands of 924 threaded onto a size 10 embroidery needle, pad the outer edge with stem stitch.

2. Using one strand of the same thread on the same needle, cover the padding with buttonhole stitch formed with the ridge on the outer edge.

3. Couch a line of Madeira Metallic 442 in the ditch between the blocks and the outer edge.

The two remaining petals have five horizontal rows of blocks. Starting from the top row, working from left to right the threads you should use are as listed in the table below:

3685	3689	3013	3835
3836	738	3685	Ecru
3013	3687	926	3790
928	3834	3012	3689
3687	3013	Ecru	3835

4. Fill the small circle in the centre with basic single weaving using Special Dentelles 738 for the warp threads and Special Dentelles Ecru for the weft threads.

5. Using two strands of 926 threaded onto a size 10 embroidery needle, pad the outer circle with stem stitch.

6. Using one strand of the same thread on the same needle, cover the padding with buttonhole stitch formed with the ridge on the outer edge.

7. Couch a line of Madeira Metallic 442 outside the ridge of the buttonhole stitch in the ditch between the outer circle and the petals.

8. Using a strand of Ecru threaded onto a size 10 embroidery needle, come up in the ditch between the two circles.

9. Pick up 15 x size 15°196 beads.

10. Take the needle back through the first 3 beads to form a circle.

11. Tighten the thread, manipulating it so that the circle of beads lies over the ditch between the two stitched circles.

12. Go down, through the fabric and thereafter come up between each bead and couch over the thread that is holding them. Take care to manipulate the beads into a neat circle as you go along.

The outer edge of each of the petals is filled with padded buttonhole stitch.

Flower 3 (grape and gold)

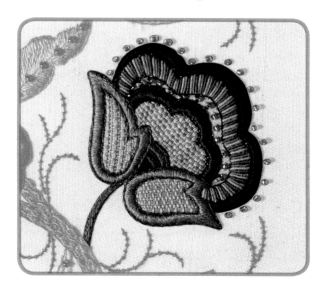

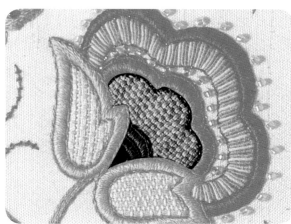

1. Fill the upper, woven, section with check and stripes no. 7. Use Special Dentelles 397 for shade 1 and Special Dentelles Ecru for shade 2.

2. The wedge below consists of 3 separate sections. Fill each of them with padded buttonhole stitch.

3. Using two strands of cotton threaded onto a size 10 embroidery needle, pad the semi-circle with stem stitch.

4. Using one strand of the same thread on the same needle, cover the padding with buttonhole stitch formed with the ridge on the upper edge.

5. Start at the top using 3835. Moving to the middle, use 3834 and make sure that this ridge of the buttonhole stitch covers the raw edge of the section above it. Using 154, fill the bottom wedge taking care, once again, to cover the raw edge of the previous section.

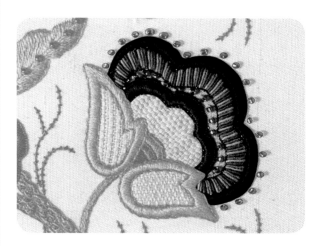

6. Using two strands of 3834 threaded onto a size 10 embroidery needle, pad the semi-circle with stem stitch.

7. Using one strand of the same thread on the same needle, cover the padding with buttonhole stitch formed with the ridge on the upper edge.

8. Outline the top and bottom edges by couching a line of *Fils Métallisé* 4270 into place.

9. Pad the striped section with two layers of stem stitch using 2 strands of 3835.

10. Cover the padding with vertical bullion knots that are made with one strand of thread on a size 10 straw needle. Fan out over the shape.

11. Use 3835 followed by Ecru and then 3053, repeating this sequence until the shape is complete.

12. Outline the bottom edge by couching a line of *Fils Métallisé* 4270 into place.

13. Stitch single beads 15°1650 at intervals in the gap between the bullion knots and the padded buttonhole stitch. Use a single strand of Ecru threaded onto a size 10 bead embroidery needle and doubled over to create a double strand.

14. Using two strands of 154 threaded onto a size 10 embroidery needle, pad the semi-circle with stem stitch.

15. Using one strand of the same thread on the same needle, cover the padding with buttonhole stitch formed with the ridge on the upper edge.

16. Stitch single beads 15°196 at intervals above and adjacent to the padded buttonhole stitch. Use a single strand of Ecru threaded onto a size 10 bead embroidery needle and doubled over to create a double strand.

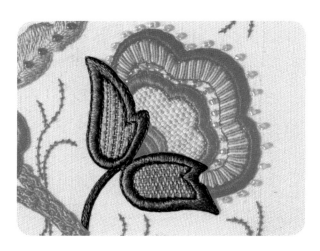

17. Fill the centre of the bottom leaves with texture no. 2 using Special Dentelles Ecru for the warp threads and Special Dentelles 738 for the weft threads.

18. Using two strands of 3053 threaded onto a size 10 embroidery needle, pad the outer edge of each leaf with stem stitch.

19. Using one strand of the same thread on the same needle, cover the padding with satin stitch. Start at the tip with a straight stitch that goes in at the tip of the weaving. Thereafter, fan the stitches so that when you reach the bottom of each leaf the stitches are facing in the opposite direction and are at right angles to the weaving.

20. Outline the outer edge of each leaf with a line of stem stitch worked with 3051.

21. Using the same thread, stitch a line of stem stitch in the ditch between the weaving and the other edge of each leaf.

22. Using 1 strand of 3790 on a size 10 embroidery needle, do a row of stem stitch up the outer line on the inside curve of the branch.

23. Now stitch back down, still doing stem stitch, immediately adjacent to the line you have just stitched. Continue doing these adjacent lines of stem stitch until you have filled the branch.

24. Outline the inner curve of the branch with stem stitch using 1 strand of 3781 on a size 10 embroidery needle.

Flower 4 (small flower)

5. Fill the three crescents with padded buttonhole stitch. The padding should be done with two strands of the relevant colour whereas the buttonhole stitch should be worked with 1 strand.

6. Starting at the top, work the first section with 928.

7. Moving to the next section, fill this with 927, making sure that the ridge of the buttonhole stitch lies over the raw edges of the section above it.

8. Fill the bottom section using 926, once again making sure that the ridge of the buttonhole stitch lies over the raw edges of the section above it.

1. Fill each of these petals with long and short stitch shading. Start with 3803 at the base of the petal, shading out to 739 at the tip.

2. Outline each petal with couching stitch using *Fils Métallisé* 4018.

3. Using a strand of 3685 threaded onto a size 10 embroidery needle, come up in the middle of each of the circles that come out of the top of the flower.

4. Pick up a size 8°645 and a size 15°313 bead. Return through the large bead leaving the smaller bead to hold it in place.

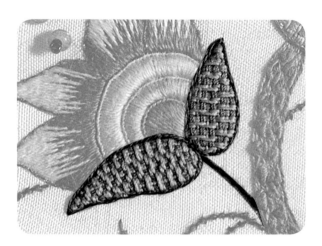

9. Fill the inside of the calyx leaves with texture no. 1 found in the Stitch Gallery.

10. Use Special Dentelles 369 for the warp threads and Special Dentelles 3052 for the weft.

11. Outline each of the leaves with stem stitch using 1 strand of 3051 threaded onto a size 10 embroidery needle.

12. The stem is a line of whipped stem stitch done with 3781.

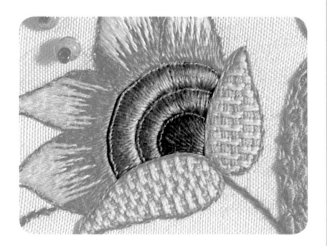

Flower 5 (far left)

1. Fill the centre of this flower with long and short stitch.

2. Start at the base with 1 strand of 3685 threaded onto a size 10 embroidery needle, shading up through 3803 and 3687 to 3688.

3. Shade back through 3687 and 3803 to 3685 at the top.

4. Do Trellis Couching with Cross Stitch Filling over the shaded area. Use 3685 for shade 1 and *Fils Métallisé* 4018 for shade 2.

5. Referring to the needle weaving stitches in the Stitch Gallery fill the centre of these petals with the stitch referred to as check and stripes no. 2.

6. Use Special Dentelles 3688 for shade 1 and Special Dentelles Ecru for shade 2.

7. Use a size 7 embroidery needle to work the warp threads and a size 26 tapestry needle for the weft threads.

8. Using stem stitch, pad the outer section of each petal with two strands of 3053 threaded onto a size 7 embroidery needle.

9. Cover the padding with satin stitch using 1 strand of 3053 threaded onto a size 10 needle. Start in the centre at the tip of the petal fanning your stitches around the shape.

10. Using 1 strand of 3051 threaded onto a size 10 embroidery needle, do a line of stem stitch around the outer edge of each petal.

11. Using the same thread, stitch a line of stem stitch in the ditch between the woven area and the outer satin stitched edge.

12. Fill the middle section on each side of the fruit with basic single weaving. Use Special Dentelles 738 or the warp threads and Special Dentelles Ecru for the weft threads.

13. Fill the outer section on each side with padded buttonhole stitch.

14. Use 2 strands of 738 threaded onto a size 7 embroidery needle and work stem stitch for the padding.

15. Change to 1 strand of the same thread on a size 10 embroidery needle and do fine buttonhole stitch over the padding. The ridge of the buttonhole stitch should face to the outer edge.

16. Fill the inner section on each side with padded buttonhole stitch.

17. Use 2 strands of Ecru threaded onto a size 7 embroidery needle and work stem stitch for the padding.

18. Change to 1 strand of the same thread on a size 10 embroidery needle and do fine buttonhole stitch over the padding. The ridge of the buttonhole stitch should face to the inner edge.

19. Couch a line of Madeira Metallic 425 into the ditch on either side of the weaving. Continue the line on the outer edge to cover the raw edge of the outer buttonhole section to the tip.

20. Referring to the needle weaving stitches in the Stitch Gallery fill the calyx at the bottom of this flower with the stitch referred to as texture no. 9.

21. Use Special Dentelles 369 for shade 1 and Special Dentelles 3052 for shade 2.

22. Outline the calyx with backstitch using 1 strand of 3051 threaded onto a size 10 embroidery needle.

23. Whip the backstitch with *Fils Métallisé* 4052 threaded onto a size 26 tapestry needle.

24. Using 3051 fill each of the leaves with raised herringbone stitch.

25. Outline each leaf with fine stem stitch using the same thread.

26. Using a strand of 3685 threaded onto a size 10 embroidery needle, come up in the middle of the circle.

27. Pick up a size 8°645 and a size 15°313 bead. Return through the large bead leaving the smaller bead to hold it in place.

28. Bring your needle up adjacent to the large bead.

29. Pick up 9 x size 11°313 beads.

30. Take the needle back through the first 3 beads to form a circle.

31. Tighten the thread, manipulating it so that the circle of beads lies around the larger bead in the middle.

32. Go down, through the fabric and thereafter come up between each bead and couch over the thread that is holding them. Take care to manipulate the beads into a neat circle as you go along.

Stems, tendrils and leaves

1. Fill the centre of these leaves with check and stripes no. 8. Use Special Dentelles 397 for shade 1 and Special Dentelles Ecru for shade 2.

2. Using 1 strand of 3011 threaded onto a size 10 embroidery needle, do a line of chain stitch adjacent to the edge of the weaving.

3. Using 1 strand of 3013 threaded onto a size 10 embroidery needle, do a line of chain stitch on the outside edge of the outer section of the leaf.

4. Fill in the remaining area with rows of chain stitch using 1 strand of 3011, 3012 and 3013 shading from dark on the inner edge through medium to light khaki green on the outer edge.

5. Outline the weaving by couching a line of *Fils Métallisé* 4270 into place.

6. Using 1 strand of 3011 threaded onto a size 10 embroidery needle, work an intermittent stem stitch outline on the outer edge of the leaf.

7. Each of these leaves is filled with diagonally worked long and short stitch shading. Use 1 strand of thread on a size 10 embroidery needle throughout.

8. For each leaf, start with the shade closest to the vein using 3013 shading out to 3836 for the light mauve leaf, 3687 for the pink leaf, 926 for the darker blue grey leaves and 927 for the lighter blue grey leaves.

9. Thread a size 10 bead embroidery needle with 1 strand of 3011, double it over and knot the two ends together.

10. Stitch single 15°459 beads at evenly spaced intervals up the vein and where needed beyond the tips of the leaves.

11. Using 1 strand of 3011 threaded onto a size 10 embroidery needle, work an intermittent stem stitch outline on the outer edge of the leaf.

12. The main branch is done in the same way throughout this design.

13. Using 3790, start a section of branch by doing a row of stem stitch up the outer line on one side.

14. Now stitch back down, still doing stem stitch, immediately adjacent to the line you have just stitched. Every now and then, instead of doing a stem stitch, do a bullion knot, and then continue stem stitching as before.

15. Continue doing these adjacent lines of stem stitch, substituting with bullions from time to time. It is these bullion knots that give the branch its gnarled appearance.

16. You should not be tempted, however, to do too many bullion knots and those that you do should be fairly evenly spread over each section of the branch.

17. Once you have completed the 'stem stitch', using 1 strand of 3781, place a French knot here and there to add more texture to the branch.

18. Stitch the curling tendrils with coral stitch using 1 strand of 3834 on a size 10 embroidery needle.

Pertinacity

CIRCULAR JACOBEAN PANEL

Dimensions: 330 mm (13") diameter

The original of this design has been specifically designed for the Sudberry House Louis XV Carved Round Footstool. It can be purchased online and website details appear in the Buyer's Guide at the back of this book. It can, however, be framed or used as a cushion panel. The line drawing for this design can be found at the back of the book and should be photocopied to size.

Materials

FABRIC

500 x 500 mm (20 x 20") Ecru Hopsack
500 x 500 mm (20 x 20") cotton voile backing fabric

NEEDLES

Size 7 Embroidery Needles x 4
Size 26 Tapestry Needles x 4
Size 28 Tapestry Needle x 1
Size 10 Embroidery Needles x 2
Size 9 Long Darner or Straw Needle x 1

THREADS

DMC STRANDED COTTON

1 skein each of

0422	Light Hazelnut Brown
0520	Dark Fern Green
0522	Fern Green
0523	Light Fern Green
0524	Very Light Fern Green
0642	Dark Beige Grey
0644	Medium Beige Grey
0677	Light Old Gold
0779	Dark Cocoa
0822	Light Beige Grey
0869	Very Dark Hazelnut Brown
0930	Dark Antique Blue
0931	Medium Antique Blue
0932	Light Antique Blue
0934	Black Avocado Green
3011	Dark Khaki Green
3012	Medium Khaki Green
3013	Light Khaki Green
3021	Very Dark Brown Grey
3041	Medium Antique Violet
3042	Light Antique Violet
3051	Dark Green Grey
3052	Medium Green Grey
3053	Light Green Grey
3740	Dark Antique Violet
3743	Very Light Antique Violet
3750	Very Dark Antique Blue
3787	Dark Brown Grey
3828	Hazelnut Brown
3860	Cocoa
3861	Light Cocoa

2 skeins of

0640	Very Dark Beige Grey

ANCHOR STRANDED COTTON
1 skein each of

0068	Mauve	3687
0069	Dark Mauve	3803
0070	Dark Garnet	0814
0072	Very Dark Garnet	0814
1028	Very Dark Mauve	3685

DMC PERLE NO. 12 THREAD
10 to 20 metres each of

0437	Light Tan
0524	Very Light Fern Green
0814	Dark Garnet
0822	Light Beige Grey
0931	Medium Antique Blue
3042	Light Antique Violet

CHAMELEON THREADS PERLE NO. 12
1 skein of

97	Green Olives

DMC LIGHT EFFECTS METALLIC THREAD
1 skein of

E436	Old Gold

DMC ART. 278 *FILS MÉTALLISÉ*
10 to 20 metres each of

4018	Metallic Bright Pink
4270	Metallic Purple Black

MADEIRA METALLIC: ART. 9842 NO. 40
10 metres of

442	Steel Black

STITCH INSTRUCTIONS
The design has been divided into sections. Each section is described in detail.

Blue leaf 1

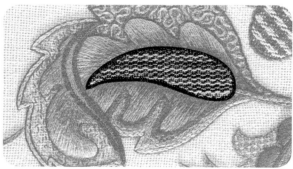

4. Once you have completed the blue shading that surrounds the weaving, work a line of backstitch in the ditch between the two areas using 2 strands of 3750 threaded onto a size 7 embroidery needle.

5. Using 1 strand of the same thread on a size 26 tapestry needle, whip the backstitch in a continuous line.

6. Using 1 strand of Madeira metallic thread colour 442 threaded onto a size 7 embroidery needle, work a line of stem stitch just inside the whipped backstitch.

TIP

To prevent snarling and twisting run both metallic and perle threads through a thread conditioner before you thread them onto a needle.

7. Working from the tip to the base of the shape and using the colour image on the left as your guide, shade this area with long and short stitch.

8. In each instance use 1 strand of thread threaded onto a size 10 embroidery needle.

9. Working from the inside, adjacent to the woven area, start with 930, shading through 931 to 932 on the right. Use the same colour sequence on the left, shading through to 3861 for the two pink areas.

10. When you have completed the vermicelli couched area on the right of the shading, work a line of backstitch on the outer edge of the right side shad-

1. Following the instructions for check and stripes no. 4 in the needle weaving section of the Stitch Gallery use Perle no. 12 524 threaded onto a size 7 embroidery needle for colour 1 and Perle no. 12 931 threaded onto a size 7 embroidery needle for colour 2.

2. Work the warp threads, according to the diagram in the Stitch Gallery, from the tip of the shape to the base.

3. Thereafter, using the same threads threaded onto size 26 tapestry needles, weave the weft threads through the warp threads according to the pattern.

ing using 2 strands of 3750 threaded onto a size 7 embroidery needle.

11. Using 1 strand of the same thread on a size 26 tapestry needle, whip the backstitch in a continuous line.

12. The area outside the left side blue shading should be filled with lines of chain stitch.

13. Using 2 strands of 520 threaded onto a size 7 embroidery needle, work a line of chain stitch immediately adjacent to the edge of the blue shading.

14. Using the colour image on the left as your guide, work a second line in the wider areas.

15. Using 2 strands of 524 threaded onto a size 7 embroidery needle, work a line of chain stitch on the outside line of this area.

16. Work a second, shorter line, and a third, even shorter line in the wider area.

17. Using 2 strands of 522 threaded onto a size 7 embroidery needle, fill the remaining space with lines of chain stitch.

18. Using 1 strand of 934 threaded onto a size 10 embroidery needle, work a line of fine stem stitch along the outer edge of this area, immediately adjacent to the lightest green chain stitch.

19. This section of the leaf is filled with vermicelli couching.

20. Following the directions in the Stitch Gallery for this stitch, thread 2 strands of 522 onto a size 7 embroidery needle and 1 strand of 522 onto a size 10 embroidery needle.

21. Come up with the 2-strand needle at any edge.

22. Using the 1-strand needle, couch the 2-strand thread into random reasonably large swirls that don't cross each other and cover the area evenly. Go into the fabric when you reach the edges, coming up further along on the edge again, trying to keep the pattern of the swirls going.

23. Once you have covered the area, thread 1 strand each of 520 onto two size 10 embroidery needles.

24. Use one of the needles to couch the thread of the other needle into smaller swirls that fit between the lighter, larger swirls. Make sure that the darker swirls are not touching the lighter ones.

25. Work a line of backstitch on the outer edge of this section using 2 strands of 934 threaded onto a size 7 embroidery needle.

26. Using 1 strand of the same thread on a size 26 tapestry needle, whip the backstitch in a continuous line.

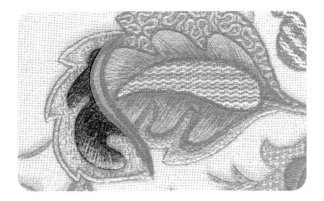

27. The area highlighted in the image on the left is filled with long and short stitch shading.

28. In each instance use 1 strand of thread threaded onto a size 10 embroidery needle.

29. Working from the base, adjacent to the vein, start with 931, shading through 3860 to 3861 and finally 822 where you still have space.

30. When you have completed the seeded area above and the vein below, work a line of fine stem stitch on the outer edge using 1 strand of 934 threaded onto a size 10 embroidery needle.

31. Fill this area with seeding.

32. Using 1 strand of 520 threaded onto a size 10 embroidery needle, work in the space that hugs the shaded area below it.

33. Change to 1 strand of 523 threaded onto a size 10 embroidery needle to work the seeding in the area closer to the edges of the section.

34. Using 2 strands of 524 threaded onto a size 7

embroidery needle, work a line of chain stitch along the outer edge of this area, working a second, shorter line in the thicker part where it meets the vein on the left.

35. Using 1 strand of 934 threaded onto a size 10 embroidery needle, work a line of fine stem stitch on each side of and adjacent to the chain stitch.

36. Using 2 strands of 3750 threaded onto a size 26 tapestry needle, work a line of heavy chain stitch on each of the outer lines of the vein.

37. Using 1 strand of 3861 threaded onto a size 10 embroidery needle, work rows of stem stitch up and down the area until you have filled it with colour.

38. Using 1 strand of Madeira metallic thread colour 442, threaded onto a size 7 embroidery needle, create a slight sparkle by working a line of stem stitch around the pink area, just inside the heavy chain stitch.

Blue leaf 2

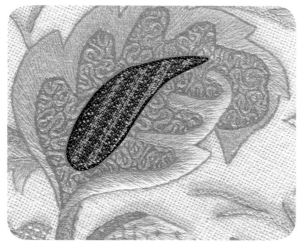

in the ditch between the two areas using 2 strands of 3750 threaded onto a size 7 embroidery needle.

5. Using 1 strand of the same thread on a size 26 tapestry needle, whip the backstitch in a continuous line.

6. Using 1 strand of Madeira metallic thread colour 442 threaded onto a size 7 embroidery needle, work a line of stem stitch just inside the whipped backstitch.

TIP

If you are finding it difficult to understand a stitch instruction, try to work through each step on a scrap of fabric. The penny will probably drop and when it does you should continue to practise until it is firmly ingrained in your fingers and your head.

1. Following the instructions for check and stripes no. 4 in the needle weaving section of the Stitch Gallery use Perle no. 12 524 threaded onto a size 7 embroidery needle for colour 1 and Perle no. 12 931 threaded onto a size 7 embroidery needle for colour 2.

2. Work the warp threads, according to the diagram in the Stitch Gallery, from the tip of the shape to the base.

3. Thereafter, using the same threads threaded onto size 26 tapestry needles, weave the weft threads through the warp threads according to the pattern.

4. Once you have completed the blue vermicelli couching that surrounds the weaving, work a line of backstitch

7. This section of the leaf is filled with vermicelli couching.

8. Following the directions in the Stitch Gallery for this stitch, thread 2 strands of 932 onto a size 7 embroidery needle and 1 strand of 932 onto a size 10 embroidery needle.

9. Come up with the 2-strand needle at any edge.

10. Using the 1-strand needle, couch the 2-strand thread into random, reasonably large swirls that don't cross each other, and cover the area evenly. Go into the fabric when you reach the edges, coming up further along on the edge again, trying to keep the pattern of the swirls going.

11. Once you have covered the area, thread 1 strand each of 3750 onto two size 10 embroidery needles.

12. Use one of the needles to couch the thread of the other needle into smaller swirls that fit between the lighter, larger swirls. Make sure that the darker swirls are not touching the lighter ones.

13. After you have completed the green shaded area, work a line of backstitch on the outer edge of this section using 2 strands of 3750 threaded onto a size 7 embroidery needle.

14. Using 1 strand of the same thread on a size 26 tapestry needle, whip the backstitch in a continuous line.

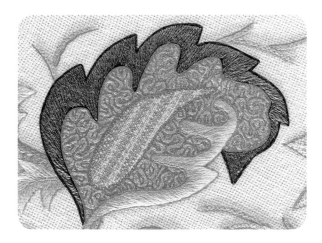

15. Starting at the tip of this area and working round to the base adjacent to the stem, fill the outer edge of this leaf with diagonal long and short stitch shading.

16. In each instance, use 1 strand of thread on a size 10 embroidery needle.

17. Working from the inside, adjacent to inner areas of this leaf, start with 522, shading through 523 to 3861 on the outer edge.

18. Work an outline of fine stem stitch on the outer edge using 1 strand of 934 threaded onto a size 10 embroidery needle.

19. Pad this area with rows of stem stitch using 4 strands of 3861 threaded onto a size 7 embroidery needle.

20. Using the image as your guide, fill this area with diagonal long and short stitch, starting with 3860 in the darker areas, shading through 3861 to 822 in the light areas.

21. Work an outline of fine stem stitch around the entire edge using 1 strand of 779 threaded onto a size 10 embroidery needle.

Large red check flower

1. Referring to check and stripes no. 2 in the needle weaving section of the Stitch Gallery, use Perle no. 12 814 threaded onto a size 7 embroidery needle for colour 1 and Perle no. 12 822 also threaded onto a size 7 embroidery needle for colour 2.

2. Working from top to bottom, do the warp threads using the Stitch Gallery along with the image above as your reference.

3. Rethread colours 1 and 2 onto size 26 tapestry needles and weave the weft threads according to the Stitch Gallery.

4. Work a line of backstitch on the outer edge of each petal using 2 strands of 72 threaded onto a size 7 embroidery needle.

5. Using 1 strand of the same thread on a size 26 tapestry needle, whip the backstitch in a continuous line.

6. Using 1 strand of the *Fils Métallisé* metallic thread 4018 on a size 7 embroidery needle, work a stem stitch outline around the whipped backstitch.

TIP

To minimise shredding when using metallic threads use a larger needle than you might otherwise have chosen. This opens up a wider channel that allows the thread to slide through the fabric with less damage.

7. Each of these leaves is padded with one to four layers of stem stitch using the thread that you use for each leaf.

8. Start by doing a layer of stem stitch over the entire leaf.

9. Do a second layer of stem stitch on the top three quarters of the leaf.

10. Do a third layer of stem stitch over the top half of the leaf.

11. Do a fourth layer of stem stitch over the top quarter of the leaf.

12. As you work each layer of stem stitch try to make sure that it forms a gradual rise in the padding as opposed to a step up as you add each layer.

13. Starting at the tip of each leaf with vertical satin stitch, cover the padding slowly fanning the stitches until they become diagonal satin stitch.

14. Working from the left, the first leaf is worked with 3053, followed by 3052, then 524 and finally the leaf on the far right should be worked with 3053.

15. Use 1 strand of thread on a size 10 needle in each instance.

16. Using 2 strands of 934 on a size 9 darner or a straw needle, work a long bullion knot to cover the vein of each leaf. You will need to wind between 65 and 75 twists on the needle when making the bullion knot.

17. Using 1 strand of 934 threaded onto a size 10 embroidery needle, loosely couch the bullion knots into the curve that they need to have to cover each vein.

18. When you have completed the stitching in the areas that surround these leaves, outline each one with a line of stem stitch using 3051 threaded onto a size 10 embroidery needle.

19. Working from the bottom row upwards, pad each of the semi-circle shapes with horizontal satin stitch using two strands of cotton on a size 10 embroidery needle.

20. Thereafter, cover the padding with satin stitch using 1 strand of the same thread.

21. Use 72 for the three shapes in the first row, 70 for the five shapes in the second, 1028 for the four shapes in the third and 69 for the three semi-circles in the top row.

22. When you have completed the stitching in the areas that surround these shapes, outline each semi-circle with fine stem stitch using 1 strand of 72 threaded onto a size 10 embroidery needle.

23. Referring to check and stripes no. 5 in the needle weaving section of the Stitch Gallery, use Perle no. 12 524 threaded onto a size 7 embroidery needle for colour 1 and Perle no. 12 822 also threaded onto a size 7 embroidery needle for colour 2.

24. The pattern of this weaving variation does not fill the space completely and you need to take this into account when working each leaf.

25. Start working the warp threads in the middle of the leaf by stitching two colour 2 threads from the pointed tip to the middle of the base of the leaf.

26. Thereafter work colour 1 warp threads on either side of the two in the centre.

27. Transferring each of the threads onto a size 26 tapestry needle, weave the weft threads following the pattern of the weave in the Stitch Gallery and taking into account that you need to count out from the two colour 2 warp threads in the middle to determine at which point you begin your weaving pattern.

28. Once you have completed the weaving, using 1 strand of 3051 on a size 28 tapestry needle, accentuate the green in the weave. Enhance the warp threads first.

29. Following the pattern that you already have in place, weave a line down the left side of the colour 2 pair of stitches in the middle of the leaf. Weave another line down the right of the colour 2 pair of stitches in the middle.

30. Thereafter, weave a line down the right hand side of the 5th green warp thread on the right of the centre and down the left hand side of the 5th green warp thread on the left of the centre.

31. Moving to enhancing the weft threads, still following the pattern that you have in place, weave a line below the bottom thread and another above the top thread on each group of green threads.

32. Work a line of backstitch on the outer edge of each petal using 2 strands of 3051 threaded onto a size 7 embroidery needle.

33. Using 1 strand of the same thread on a size 26 tapestry needle, whip the backstitch in a continuous line.

34. Pad each of the petals that rise out of the calyx with horizontal satin stitch using 2 strands of 822 threaded onto a size 7 embroidery needle.

35. Cover the padding with long and short stitch shading using 1 strand of thread on a size 10 embroidery needle.

36. Working from base to tip, use 644 shading up to 822 for the middle petal.

37. Working, once again, from base to tip, use 642 shading into 644 for the petals on either side of the centre.

38. Outline the outer edge of each petal with fine stem stitch using 3787 threaded onto a size 10 embroidery needle.

39. Fill each of the five green leaves below the petals with a line of extended fly stitch. Leave a small gap between the side arms of the fly stitch. Fill these gaps with straight stitches in a darker colour, burying the end of each stitch under the ridge of the fly stitch.

40. Using 2 strands of thread on a size 7 embroidery needle in each instance, work the centre leaf using 3053 for the fly stitch and 524 for the straight stitch.

41. The leaves on either side of that one are worked using 3052 for the fly stitch and 3053 for the straight stitch.

42. Use 3051 for the fly stitch and 3052 for the straight stitch when you work the two outside leaves.

43. Outline each leaf with fine stem stitch using 1 strand of 934 threaded onto a size 10 embroidery needle.

44. Pad the circle at the base of the leaves with horizontal satin stitch using 2 strands of thread on a size 7 embroidery needle.

45. Cover the padding with vertical satin stitch using 1 strand of the same thread.

Small red check flower

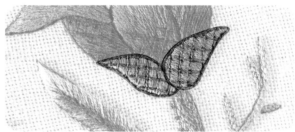

1. Fill the two green leaves that form the calyx with stem stitch padding using 2 strands of 3053 on a size 7 embroidery needle.

2. Cover the padding with vertical satin stitch using the same thread.

3. Do basic trellis couching over the satin stitch using 1 strand of 3051 on a size 10 embroidery needle.

4. When you have completed the red petals above the calyx, outline each green leaf with stem stitch using 1 strand of 3051 on a size 10 embroidery needle.

5. Work each of the red petals individually.

6. The outside petals are worked in the same way.

7. Using 2 strands of 70 on a size 7 embroidery needle, pad the bottom half of the lower section with vertical rows of stem stitch.

8. Cover that padding with long and short stitch shading, starting at the base with 72, shading through 70 up to 1028 at the top. Use 1 strand of thread on a size 10 embroidery needle in each instance.

9. Using the image as your guide, do intermittent basic trellis couching in the top half of this section using 1 strand of 72 on a size 10 embroidery needle.

10. Using 2 strands of 822 on a size 7 embroidery needle, pad the upper section with rows of stem stitch that start at the base and go towards the tip. Work a second layer with 1028 on the inside half of the upper section.

11. Cover that padding with long and short stitch shading, starting at the base with 1028, shading through 69 and 68 up to 524 at the tip. Use 1 strand of thread on a size 10 embroidery needle in each instance.

12. Using 2 strands of 822 on a size 7 embroidery needle, pad the centre petal with stem stitch. Changing to 1028, work a second layer of padding in the bottom two thirds of the petal. Changing to 70, work a third layer of padding in the bottom third of the petal.

13. As you work each layer of stem stitch try to make sure that it forms a gradual rise in the padding as opposed to a step up as you add each layer.

14. Cover that padding with long and short stitch shading, starting at the base with 72, shading through

70, 1028, 69 and 68 up to 524 at the tip. Use 1 strand of thread on a size 10 embroidery needle in each instance.

15. When you have completed the surrounding embroidery, using the colour image as your guide, do intermittent outlines on about half of the outside perimeter of each section of each petal with stem stitch using 1 strand of 72 on a size 10 embroidery needle.

16. Changing to 1 strand of the *Fils Métallisé* metallic thread 4018 on a size 7 embroidery needle, work stem stitch in the sections of the perimeters not already outlined by the darker red cotton.

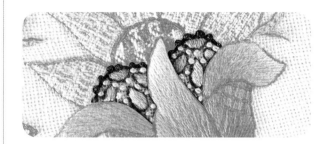

17. Using 2 strands of thread on a size 7 embroidery needle, pad each of the shapes in this section with horizontal satin stitch. Thereafter, with 1 strand of the same thread on a size 10 embroidery needle, cover the padding with vertical satin stitch.

18. Use 3828 for the circle 'centre' of the daisy and 422 for the teardrop 'petals'.

19. Outline each of these shapes with stem stitch using 1 strand of 869.

20. Using 2 strands of 822 on a size 7 embroidery needle, work evenly spaced French knots over the remaining area.

21. When you have stitched the areas around this section, outline the top with stem stitch using 2 strands of 934 on a size 7 embroidery needle.

22. Using the same thread, work French knots at intervals on the outside edge of the stem stitch outline.

23. Referring to check and stripes no. 2 in the needle weaving section of the Stitch Gallery, use Perle no. 12 814 threaded onto a size 7 embroidery needle for colour 1 and Perle no. 12 822 also threaded onto a size 7 embroidery needle for colour 2.

24. Working from top to bottom, do the warp threads using the Stitch Gallery along with the image on the left as your reference.

25. Rethread colours 1 and 2 onto size 26 tapestry needles and weave the weft threads according to the Stitch Gallery.

26. When you have stitched the areas around this section, work a backstitch outline on the upper edge of the semi-circle using 2 strands of 72 threaded onto a size 7 embroidery needle.

27. Using 1 strand of the same thread on a size 26 tapestry needle, whip the backstitch in a continuous line.

28. Using 1 strand of the *Fils Métallisé* metallic thread 4018 on a size 7 embroidery needle, work a stem stitch line in the ditch between the whipped backstitch and the woven checks.

29. Referring to check and stripes no. 5 in the needle weaving section of the Stitch Gallery, use Perle no. 12 524 threaded onto a size 7 embroidery needle for colour 1 and Perle no. 12 822 also threaded onto a size 7 embroidery needle for colour 2.

30. The pattern of this weaving variation does not fill the space completely and you need to take this into account when working each leaf.

31. Start working the warp threads in the middle of the leaf by stitching two colour 2 threads from the pointed tip to the middle of the base of the leaf.

32. Thereafter work colour 1 warp threads on either side of the two in the centre.

33. Transferring each of the threads onto a size 26 tapestry needle, weave the weft threads following the pattern of the weave in the Stitch Gallery and taking into account that you need to count out from the two colour 2 warp threads in the middle to determine at which point you begin your weaving pattern.

34. Once you have completed the weaving, using 1 strand of 3051 on a size 28 tapestry needle, accentuate the green in the weave. Enhance the warp threads first.

35. Following the pattern that you already have in place, weave a line down the left side of the colour 2 pair of stitches in the middle of the leaf. Weave another line down the right of the colour 2 pair of stitches in the middle.

36. Thereafter, weave a line down the right hand side of the 5th green warp thread on the right of the centre and down the left hand side of the 5th green warp thread on the left of the centre.

37. Now moving to enhancing the weft threads, still following the pattern that you have in place, weave a line below the bottom thread and another above the top thread on each group of green threads.

38. Work a line of backstitch on the outer edge of each petal using 2 strands of 3051 threaded onto a size 7 embroidery needle.

39. Using 1 strand of the same thread on a size 26 tapestry needle, whip the backstitch in a continuous line.

Large purple flower

1. Each of these woven petals is worked in the same way following the instructions for check and stripes no. 10 in the Stitch Gallery.

2. The Chameleon and DMC Perle no. 12 threads you should use are as follows: colour 1 Chameleon 97, colour 2 DMC 822, colour 3 DMC 524, Colour 4 DMC 3042. Use the same sequence of colours for both the warp and weft threads. Use a size 7

embroidery needle for each thread when working the warp stitches, changing to a size 26 tapestry needle when you weave the weft threads.

3. Start in the middle of the shape with colour no. 1, working out to each side following the colour sequence. When you reach the end of the shape on any particular side, do not be concerned if your petal is not identical to the image. Everyone's tension and spacing is different.

4. Using 1 strand of the *Fils Métallisé* metallic thread 4270 on a size 26 tapestry needle, accentuate the purple in the weave. Enhance the warp threads first.

5. Following the pattern that you already have in place, weave a line down both sides of each purple thread in both the warp and weft threads.

6. When you have done the embroidery in the areas which abut the woven petals, work a line of back-stitch on the outer edge of each petal using 2 strands of 934 threaded onto a size 7 embroidery needle.

7. Using 1 strand of the same thread on a size 26 tapestry needle, whip the backstitch in a continuous line.

8. Using 1 strand of the *Fils Métallisé* metallic thread 4270 on a size 7 embroidery needle do a line of stem stitch around each petal adjacent to and on the outside of the whipped backstitch.

9. Using 2 strands of 70 on a size 7 embroidery needle, pad each of these petals separately with stem stitch.

10. Cover the padding with long and short stitch shading starting at the base of the petal with 70 shading up to 1028. In each instance, use 1 strand of cotton threaded onto a size 10 embroidery needle.

11. When you have done the embroidery in the areas that surround these petals, work a line of fine stem stitch on the outer edge of each petal using 1 strands of 72 threaded onto a size 10 embroidery needle.

12. Pad each of these semi-circles with horizontal satin stitch using 2 strands of cotton threaded onto a size 7 embroidery needle.

13. Cover the padding with fine buttonhole stitch using 1 strand of cotton on a size 10 embroidery needle. The ridge should form on the upper edge of the semi-circle.

14. Start with the row at the top using 3743. Use 3042 for the second row, 3041 for the third and 3740 for the two semi-circles at the bottom. When working the second and subsequent rows, make sure that the ridge of the buttonhole stitch lies over and masks the raw edge of the stitches in the previous row.

15. Using 1 strand of the *Fils Métallisé* metallic thread 4270 on a size 7 embroidery needle do a line of stem stitch around the outside edge of the semi-circle buttonhole shapes.

16. Start by working the main body of the berry centre. Pad each segment in vertical stem stitch using 2 strands of cotton on a size 7 embroidery needle. Using 1 strand of cotton on a size 10 embroidery needle, cover the padding with horizontal satin stitch.

17. Start with the centre segment using 644. Use 642 for the segments on either side and 640 for the two outer segments.

18. Outline the top notch with backstitch using 2 strands of 3787 on a size 7 embroidery needle.

19. Fill this area with approximately 8 flowers made up of a 10-wrap French knot in the centre surrounded by 5 drizzle stitches. The drizzle stitches that make up the lighter flowers in the centre should be made up with 7 'cast-ons', whilst the darker flowers have 5 'cast-ons' in each drizzle stitch.

20. Work the 10-wrap French knots that form the centre of each flower with 2 strands of 642 on a size 7 embroidery needle.

21. The drizzle stitches that form the petals of the lighter flowers are worked with 2 strands of 822, whilst the darker flowers use 644. Use a size 7 embroidery needle.

22. Pad the green leaves that form the calyx of the berry centre with horizontal satin stitch using 2 strands of cotton on a size 7 embroidery needle.

23. Cover the padding with satin stitch worked with 1 strand of cotton on a size 10 embroidery needle.

24. Use 520 for the centre and two outer leaves. Use 522 for the remaining shapes.

25. Pad the upper portion of the calyx with vertical stem stitch using 2 strands of 640 on a size 7 embroidery needle. Leave an empty line up the centre.

26. Cover the padding with Romanian Stitch, placing the couching stitch in the gap that you left in the padding.

27. Fill each of the three green leaves below the petals with a line of fly stitch using 2 strands of 520 on a size 7 embroidery needle. Leave a small gap between the side arms of the fly stitch.

28. Fill these gaps with straight stitches using 523 on the same size needle, burying the end of each stitch under the ridge of the fly stitch.

29. Outline each leaf with fine stem stitch using 1 strand of 934 threaded onto a size 10 embroidery needle.

30. When you have completed the branch that holds this flower, work a looped bullion knot in the ditch between the stem and the green calyx leaves. Use 2 strands of 3787 on a size 9 darner or straw needle and couch it in two places so that it stays where you want it to be.

31. Each stalk of the stamens that radiate from the top of this flower is made with a line of heavy chain stitch using 2 strands of 640 threaded onto a size 28 tapestry needle.

32. Using 1 strand of 3021 on a size 10 embroidery needle, do a line of fine stem stitch down one side of each stalk to create a shadow effect.

33. Using 2 strands of 644 on a size 7 embroidery needle, do three 2-wrap French knots around the tip of each stalk.

TIP

To make a looped bullion knot wrap the needle many times more than you need to fill the space available. This will cause it to loop.

Tartan flower 1

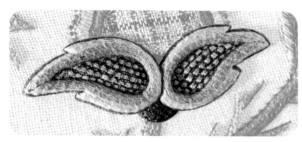

1. The inner space of these petals is filled with texture no. 2 in the needle weaving section of the Stitch Gallery.

2. Use Chameleon Threads Perle no. 12 97 threaded onto a size 7 embroidery needle for the warp stitches.

3. Use DMC Perle no. 12 524 threaded onto a size 7 embroidery needle for the weft stitches.

4. Pad the area surrounding the weaving with stem stitch using 2 strands of 422 threaded onto a size 7 embroidery needle.

5. Over the padding, work straight stitches with the same thread at right angles to the existing stitches and about 3 mm (⅛″) apart. These form the base ladder for raised stem stitch.

6. Working from the inside out and starting at the tip of the petal with 2 strands of 3828 on a size 26 tapestry needle, whip the straight stitches according to the instructions for raised stem stitch in the crewel stitches section of the Stitch Gallery.

7. Using the diagram as your guide, shade through 422 to 677 on the outer edge.

8. Using 2 strands of 869 on a size 7 embroidery needle, work a line of stem stitch in the ditch between the weaving and the raised stem stitch.

9. When you have completed the sections adjacent to the raised stem stitch, do a stem stitch outline around the perimeter of these petals using 2 strands of 869 on a size 7 embroidery needle.

10. Pad the small semi-circle at the base of the petals with horizontal satin stitch using 2 strands of 934 on a size 7 embroidery needle.

11. Cover the padding with vertical satin stitch using 1 strand of the same thread on a size 10 embroidery needle.

12. Using 1 strand of 520 on a size 10 embroidery needle, do diagonal basic trellis couching over the stitched semi-circle.

13. Outline the bottom edge of this shape with the same thread.

14. Fill the centre of this flower with check and stripes no. 11 in the needle weaving section of the Stitch Gallery.

15. Use a size 7 embroidery for each thread when working the warp stitches, changing to a size 26 tapestry needle when you weave the weft threads.

16. The Chameleon and DMC Perle no. 12 threads you should use are as follows: colour 1 DMC 814, colour 2 DMC 524, colour 3 DMC 437, Colour 4 Chameleon 97, colour 5 DMC 822. Use the same sequence of colours for both the warp and weft threads. Start in the middle of the shape with colour no. 1, working out to each side following the colour sequence.

17. Using 1 strand of the DMC Light Effects metallic thread E436 on a size 26 tapestry needle, accentuate the gold in the weave. Enhance the warp threads first.

18. Following the pattern that you already have in place, weave a line down the left side of the left 437 thread and down the right side of the right 437 thread in both the warp and weft threads.

19. When you have completed the dark green buttonhole stitch border above the tartan weave, couch 1 strand of E436 in the ditch between the two areas. Use two size 7 embroidery needles with 1 strand of the thread on each.

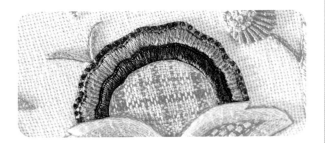

20. Pad the top section with stem stitch using 2 strands of 642 on a size 7 embroidery needle.

21. Using the same thread and with the ridge forming at the top, cover the padding with buttonhole stitch. Leave a small gap of about 1 mm (³/₆₄") between each stitch.

22. Using 644 on a size 7 embroidery needle, place a straight stitch in these gaps. Start at the base, burying the end of the stitch under the ridge of the button-hole stitch.

23. Using 520 on a size 7 embroidery needle and using the colour image as your guide, do French knots at intervals around the top of this section, adjacent to the ridge of the buttonhole stitch.

24. Using 520 on a size 7 embroidery needle, pad the section below. Using the same thread work close buttonhole stitch over the padding. The ridge should be at the top and should cover the raw edge of the stitches in the section above.

Tartan fower 2

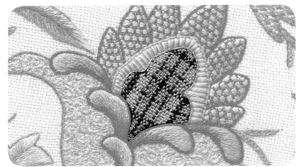

1. Fill the centre of this flower with check and stripes no. 11 in the needle weaving section of the Stitch Gallery.

2. Use a size 7 embroidery for each thread when working the warp stitches, changing to a size 26 tapestry needle when you weave the weft threads.

3. The Chameleon and DMC Perle no. 12 threads you should use are as follows: colour 1 DMC 814, colour 2 DMC 524, colour 3 DMC 437, Colour 4 Chameleon 97, colour 5 DMC 822. Use the same sequence of colours for both the warp and weft threads. Start in the middle of the shape with colour no. 1, working out to each side following the colour sequence.

4. Using 1 strand of the DMC Light Effects metallic thread E436 on a size 26 tapestry needle, accentuate the gold in the weave. Enhance the warp threads first.

5. Following the pattern that you already have in place, weave a line down the left side of the left 437 thread and down the right side of the right 437 thread in both the warp and weft threads.

6. When you have completed the buttonhole stitch border above the tartan weave, couch 1 strand of E436 in the ditch between the two areas. Use two size 7 embroidery needles with 1 strand of the thread on each.

7. The inner space of these outer petals is filled with texture no. 2 in the needle weaving section of the Stitch Gallery.

8. Use Chameleon Threads Perle no. 12 97 threaded onto a size 7 embroidery needle for the warp stitches.

9. Use DMC Perle no. 12 524 threaded onto a size 7 embroidery needle for the weft stitches.

10. Work a line of backstitch on the outer edge of each petal using 2 strands of 934 threaded onto a size 7 embroidery needle.

11. Using 1 strand of the same thread on a size 26 tapestry needle, whip the backstitch in a continuous line.

12. Using the 3828 on a size 7 embroidery needle and with the ridge forming at the top, cover the padding with buttonhole stitch. Leave a small gap of about 2 mm ($^5/_{64}$") between each stitch.

13. Using 677 and then 869, each on a size 7 embroidery needle, place straight stitches in these gaps. Start at the base, burying the end of the stitches under the ridge of the buttonhole stitch.

14. Each of these bottom petals is filled with vermicelli couching.

15. Following the directions in the Stitch Gallery for this stitch, thread 2 strands of 422 onto a size 7 embroidery needle and 1 strand of 422 onto a size 10 embroidery needle.

16. Come up with the 2-strand needle at any edge.

17. Using the 1-strand needle, couch the 2-strand thread into random reasonably large swirls that don't cross each other and cover the area evenly. Go into the fabric when you reach the edges, coming up further along on the edge again, trying to keep the pattern of the swirls going.

18. Once you have covered the area, thread 1 strand each of 3828 onto two size 10 embroidery needles.

19. Use one of the needles to couch the thread of the other needle into smaller swirls that fit between the lighter, larger swirls. Make sure that the darker swirls are not touching the lighter ones.

20. Work a line of backstitch on the outer edge of this section using 2 strands of 869 threaded onto a size 7 embroidery needle.

21. Using 1 strand of the same thread on a size 26 tapestry needle, whip the backstitch in a continuous line.

22. Using 2 strands of 522 on a size 7 embroidery needle, pad each of these shapes with stem stitch.

23. Cover the padding with long and short stitch shading using 1 strand of thread on a size 10 embroidery needle.

24. Start at the base with 520 shading through 522 to 523 at the tip.

25. Outline each shade with a line of backstitch using 2 strands of 520 threaded onto a size 7 embroidery needle.

26. Using 1 strand of the same thread on a size 26 tapestry needle, whip the backstitch in a continuous line.

Purple leaf

1. The top section of this leaf is filled with vermicelli couching.

2. Following the directions in the Stitch Gallery for this stitch, thread 2 strands of 3042 onto a size 7 embroidery needle and 1 strand of 3042 onto a size 10 embroidery needle.

3. Come up with the 2-strand needle at any edge.

4. Using the 1-strand needle, couch the 2-strand thread into random reasonably large swirls that don't cross each other and cover the area evenly. Go into the fabric when you reach the edges, coming up further along on the edge again, trying to keep the pattern of the swirls going.

5. Once you have covered the area, thread 1 strand each of 3041 onto two size 10 embroidery needles.

6. Use one of the needles to couch the thread of the other needle into smaller swirls that fit between the lighter, larger swirls. Make sure that the darker swirls are not touching the lighter ones.

7. Work a line of backstitch on the outer edge of this section using 2 strands of 3740 threaded onto a size 7 embroidery needle.

8. Using 1 strand of the same thread on a size 26 tapestry needle, whip the backstitch in a continuous line.

9. Using 1 strand of the *Fils Métallisé* metallic thread 4270 on a size 7 embroidery needle, do a line of stem stitch adjacent to and on the outside of the whipped backstitch.

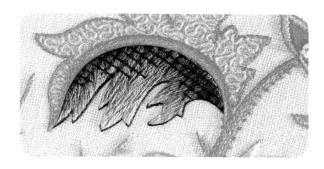

10. Using 2 strands of 822 on a size 7 embroidery needle, pad the inside three quarters of this section with stem stitch.

11. Do a second layer of padding over the inside half of this section, followed by a third layer on the inside quarter closest to the vein.

12. Cover the padding with long and short stitch shading using 1 strand of thread on a size 10 embroidery needle.

13. Start with 3051, shading through 3052, 3053 and 3743 to 822 at the tips. Use the colour image as your guide.

14. Using 1 strand of 934 on a size 10 embroidery needle, and using the colour image as your guide, do basic trellis couching over the section closest to the vein of the leaf.

15. Using the same thread, work intermittent stem stitch outlines on the outer edge of this section of the leaf.

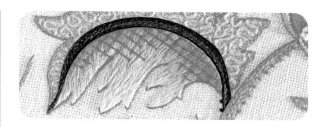

16. Using 2 strands of 640 on a size 7 embroidery needle, work a line of chain stitch along the lower edge of the vein, all the way to the tip.

17. Using 2 strands of 3787 on a size 7 embroidery needle, work a line of chain stitch for the space available along the upper edge of the vein.

18. Fill the remaining space in the middle with chain stitch using 640.

19. Outline both the lower and upper outside edges with stem stitch using 1 strand of 3021 on a size 10 embroidery needle.

Red dot leaf

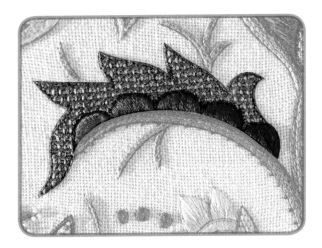

1. Pad each semi-circle with horizontal satin stitch using 2 strands of thread on a size 7 embroidery needle.

2. Using 1 strand of thread on a size 10 embroidery needle, cover the padding with vertical satin stitch, starting in the middle and fanning out ever so slightly to each side.

3. The circle at the base of the leaf is worked with 72, followed by 70, 1027, 69 and 68 at the tip.

4. When you have done the woven trellis in the outer section of the leaf, outline the upper edge of each semi-circle with stem stitch using 1 strand of 72 on a size embroidery needle.

5. When you have stitched the stem to which this leaf is attached, work a line of fine stem stitch in the ditch between the crimson semi-circles and the stem, effectively outlining that edge of the stem. Use 1 strand of 3021 on a size 10 embroidery needle.

6. Thereafter, thread 1 strand of *Fils Métallisé* metallic 4018 on a size 7 embroidery needle. Fold it over into a double strand, tying a knot to secure the two ends together.

7. Stitch two or three vertical straight stitches on top of each other at the point where the semi-circles meet one another. Start just inside the woven trellised area and finish at the edge of the vein.

8. Referring to the instructions for woven trellis couching in the crewel stitches section of the Stitch Gallery, fill this section of the leaf.

9. Use 2 strands of 3012 on a size 7 embroidery needle for shade 1.

10. Use 2 strands of 3011 on a size 7 embroidery needle for shade 2.

11. Use 2 strands of 3013 on a size 7 embroidery needle for shade 3.

12. Use the same thread on a size 26 tapestry needle for shade 4 which does the weaving.

13. Work a line of backstitch on the outer edge of this section using 2 strands of 3011 threaded onto a size 7 embroidery needle.

14. Using 1 strand of the same thread on a size 26 tapestry needle, whip the backstitch in a continuous line.

Small golden leaf

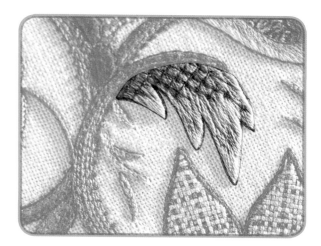

1. Using 2 strands of 822 on a size 7 embroidery needle, pad the inside three quarters of this leaf with stem stitch.

2. Do a second layer of padding over the inside half of this section, followed by a third layer on the inside quarter closest to the vein.

3. Cover the padding with long and short stitch shading using 1 strand of thread on a size 10 embroidery needle.

4. Start with 3828, shading through 422, 677 and 524 to 822 at the tips. Use the colour image as your guide.

5. Using 1 strand of 869 on a size 10 embroidery needle, and using the colour image as your guide, do

basic trellis couching over the section closest to the vein of the leaf.

6. Using the same thread, work intermittent stem-stitch outlines on the outer edge of this section of the leaf.

Small purple flowers

1. Using two strands of cotton on a size 7 embroidery needle, pad each of the purple centres of the petals with horizontal satin stitch.

2. Using 1 strand of cotton on a size 10 embroidery needle, do vertical satin stitch over the padding.

3. Use 3743 for the flower closest to the leaf that has been worked with purple vermicelli stitch. The

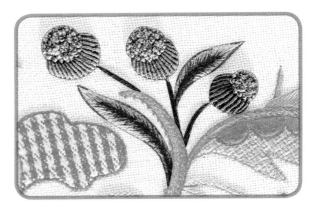

flower that sits below the purple check flower next to the red dot leaf uses 3041. Moving to the other side of the design, stitch the two flowers that are on the outer edge, and the one near the tartan flower, with 3041. Use 3042 for the remaining flower next to the blue leaf.

4. Work a continuous line of French knots around the edge of the space at the base of the 3 petals using 2 strands of 3787 on a size 7 embroidery needle.

5. In this area work a flower made up of a 10-wrap French knot in the centre surrounded by 7 drizzle stitches, each with 5 'cast-ons'.

6. Work the 10-wrap French knot with 2 strands of 642 on a size 7 embroidery needle.

7. The drizzle stitches that form the petals are worked with 2 strands of 822.

8. The green boarders around the purple centres are filled with knotted pearl stitch.

9. Use 3053 for the flower that was stitched with 3042, and use 3052 for the rest.

10. Outline both sides of the green border with stem stitch done with 3051.

11. The stems are worked with heavy chain stitch using 3787.

Blue berries

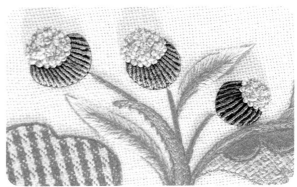

1. Fill each of these berries with whipped spider's web filling using 2 strands of cotton on a size 26 tapestry needle.

2. In each set of 3 berries, use 932 for the two larger berries and 931 for the small fruit. The berry which stands alone is done with 931.

3. Work the whipped spider's web filling from the centre to the outer edge and when complete do a long vertical straight stitch with 2 strands of cotton on a size 7 embroidery needle in the space between the ridges.

4. Use 931 for the lighter berries and 930 for the straight stitches between the ridges of the darker fruits.

Small yellow flowers

5. Blend 1 strand each of 3013, 822, 3860 and 3861 and thread this combination onto a size 7 embroidery needle.
6. Cover the centres of the berries with an even layer of 2-wrap French knots.
7. Do a second layer of knots in the centre two thirds of the shape, allowing them to lie gently on top of the previous layer.
8. Do a third layer in the centre one third of the shape.

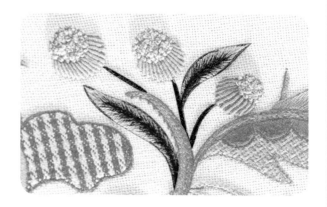

9. The colourful leaves that are found near these berries are filled with long and short stitch shading.
10. Start at the tip of each leaf with vertical stitching and slowly fan the stitches to become diagonal stitching which faces into the vein on either side.
11. Working from the inside out, start with 70 shading out to 3013 on the sides and up to 822 on the tip.
12. Using the colour image to guide you, work intermittent stem stitch outlines using 1 strand of 3011 on a size 10 embroidery needle.
13. The stems are heavy chain stitch with 3787.

1. The petals of these small flowers, which appear three times in this design, are filled with long and short stitch shading using 1 strand of thread on a size 10 embroidery needle.
2. Start at the base with 422 shading up to 677 at the tip.
3. Using the colour image to guide you, work intermittent stem stitch outlines using 1 strand of 3828 on a size 10 embroidery needle.

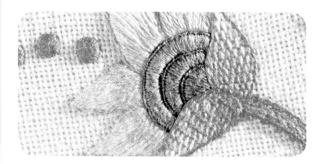

4. Pad the top semi-circle with stem stitch using 2 strands of 524 on a size 7 embroidery needle.

5. Using 1 strand of the same thread on a size 10 embroidery needle, do fine buttonhole stitch over the padding with the ridge forming at the top. Make sure that the ridge covers the raw edges at the bottom of the long and short stitch.

6. Work the middle semi-circle in the same way using 522, making sure that the ridge covers the raw edges at the bottom of the previous semi-circle.

7. Work the bottom wedge-shape in the same way using 3828, making sure that the ridge covers the raw edges at the bottom of the previous semi-circle.

8. Fill each of the petals that form the calyx with rows of buttonhole stitch. Do the stitches approximately 1 mm (³/₆₄") apart. The stitches of the second and subsequent rows should start in the middle of the gaps and just below the ridge of the previous row.

9. Using a size 7 embroidery needle throughout, start at the tip of the petal working 2 rows using 2 strands of 822.

10. Work the next 2 rows using 1 strand each of 822 and 3861.

11. Use 2 strands of 3861 for the next 2 rows.

12. Follow that with two rows that use 1 strand each of 3861 and 3860.

13. Fill in the remaining space with a row of 2 buttonhole stitches done with 2 strands of 3860.

14. When you have completed both petals, outline them individually with stem stitch using 1 strand of 779 on a size 10 embroidery needle.

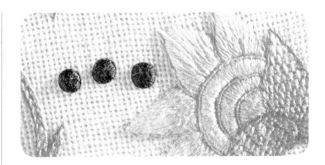

15. Using 2 strands of 779 on a size 7 embroidery needle, fill each circle with horizontal satin stitch.

16. Cover this with vertical satin stitch with 1 strand of the same thread on a size 10 embroidery needle.

Stems and tendrils

1. Stitch the brown branches, which appear throughout and form the backbone of this design, in the same way. Use the colour photographs as your guide.

2. Using 2 strands of 640 on a size 7 embroidery needle, do chain stitch on the outside line of the inside curve of the branch.

3. Using 2 strands of 3787 on a size 7 embroidery needle, do chain stitch on the outside line of the outside curve of the branch.

4. Thereafter repeat these two lines of chain stitch until you reach the middle of the branch.

5. Fill in with shorter rows in the relevant colour where necessary.

6. Using 1 strand of 3021 on a size 10 embroidery needle, work a line of stem stitch adjacent to, and touching, the lighter row of chain stitch on the inside curve of the branch.

7. Using 1 strand of the same thread work small 2-wrap French knots adjacent to, and touching the stem stitch, leaving gaps of 3 mm (⅛") between the knots.

8. Stitch the tendrils, which come off the main branches and appear throughout the design in the same way.

9. Stitch each line with heavy chain stitch.

10. Use 2 strands of thread on a size 7 embroidery needle, working some of the lines with 640 and the others with 642, to provide a little shading.

11. Using 1 strand of 3021 on a size 10 embroidery needle, work a line of stem stitch adjacent to, and touching, the inside curve of each tendril.

12. Stitch these six small leaves, which come off the main branches and appear throughout the design in the same way.

13. Fill each leaf with long and short stitch that faces into the vein, using 1 strand of thread on a size 10 embroidery needle.

14. Starting from the inside use 3012 shading through 3013 to the side and into 822 at the tips.

15. Outline each leaf with stem stitch using 1 strand of 3011 on a size 10 embroidery needle.

16. Using the same thread, work a line of stem stitch up the vein.

Dancing threads

RECTANGULAR JACOBEAN PANEL

Dimensions: 120 mm (4¾") wide by 77 mm (3") high

The original of this design has been mounted in a music box. It can be purchased online and website details appear in the Buyer's Guide at the back of this book. The line drawing for this design can be found at the back of the book and should be photocopied to size.

Materials

FABRIC

280 x 240 mm (11 x 9½") winter white dupion silk
280 x 240 mm (11 x 9½") cotton voile backing fabric

NEEDLES

Size 7 Embroidery Needles
Size 28 Tapestry Needles
Size 10 Embroidery Needles
Size 10 Bead Embroidery Needles

STITCH INSTRUCTIONS

- Use one strand of thread, unless otherwise stated.
- The design has been divided into sections. Each section is described in detail.

THREAD & BEADS

DMC STRANDED COTTON

0712	Cream
0738	Very Light Tan
0739	Ultra Very Light Tan

DMC SATIN THREAD

S739	Ultra Very Light Tan

DMC SPECIAL DENTELLES

Ecru	Ecru
0738	Very Light Tan

DMC *FILS MÉTALLISÉ*

4024	Metallic Light Gold

MIYUKI BEADS

15˚196	2g	24 carat Yellow Gold Lined Opal

Top left flower

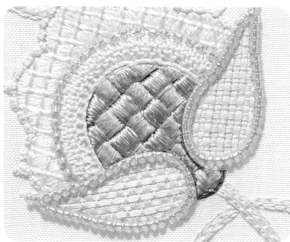

1. Each block in the centre of this section is filled with padded satin stitches, worked at right angles to one another.

2. Starting in the top left corner, use a single strand of S739 on a size 7 embroidery needle. Double it over and tie a knot at the raw end.

3. Working in a horizontal direction, do satin stitch over the block, starting and ending the stitches just inside the lines.

4. Work a small knot on the back of your work and snip just one of the 2 strands so that what is on your needle becomes a single strand.

5. Working in a vertical direction, cover the padding with satin stitch using that single strand.

6. Moving onto the next block in the top row, use a single strand of 712 on a size 10 embroidery needle. Double it over and tie a knot at the raw end.

7. Working in a vertical direction, do satin stitch over the block, starting and ending the stitches just inside the lines.

8. Work a small knot on the back of your work and snip just one of the 2 strands so that what is on your needle becomes a single strand.

9. Working in a horizontal direction, cover the padding with satin stitch using that single strand.

10. Pad the semi-circle area above the checks with stem stitch, using 2 strands of 712 on a size 7 embroidery needle.

11. Using 1 strand of the same thread on a size 10 embroidery needle, work vertical satin stitch over the padding.

12. Start in the middle at the top, fanning the stitches to the left and to the right as you work around each side.

13. With 1 strand of Dentelles Ecru on a size 28 tapestry needle, work backstitch adjacent to and just beneath the padded satin stitch.

14. Work another row adjacent to and just above the padded satin stitch.

15. Using the same thread and starting on the left of the semi-circle, work 3 rows of needle lace stitch no. 9.

16. You will finish on the right hand side.

TIP

Satin thread tends to be difficult to work with because it is bouncy and inclined to fluff easily. Pull it through a thread conditioner before you use it.

17. Attach the needle lace to the bottom row of back-stitch by bringing your needle up below the centre of the large loop that runs between the single detached buttonhole stitches in the last row of needle lace.

18. Catch the loop by going over and under its thread.

19. Go back into the fabric and bring your needle up below the centre of the next large loop.

20. When you get to the other side, come up at the beginning of the bottom row of backstitch and whip all the way back to the right hand side to cover your raw ends and to provide a border for the bottom of the needle lace.

TIP

Because it is a twisted thread, Dentelles tends to snarl up as you work the detached button-hole stitches in the needle lace technique. Pull it through a thread conditioner before you use it.

21. Fill the leaves radiating from the top of this section with diagonal satin stitch that goes into the vein on each side.

22. Start with a straight stitch at the top followed by stitches that fan around until you have reached a diagonal angle and repeat for the rest of each side.

23. Work the middle leaf in 1 strand of 712 and the two side leaves with 1 strand of 739, all threaded on a size 10 embroidery needle.

24. Using 2 strands of 712 on a size 7 embroidery needle, work vertical satin stitch over the semi-circular area of this section.

25. Start in the middle at the top fanning the stitches to the left and to the right as you work around each side.

26. Using 1 strand of S739 on a size 7 embroidery needle, work basic trellis couching over the satin stitch.

27. Do a small, barely visible couching stitch over each intersection.

28. Using 1 strand of Dentelles Ecru on a size 28 tapestry needle, do a line of large backstitch around and adjacent to the scalloped edge of the satin stitch. Make each stitch large enough to accommodate three detached buttonhole stitches.

29. Turn your embroidery around, so that you are working towards yourself.

30. Starting on the left and working with the same thread, come up through the same hole at the beginning of the backstitch.

31. Work three detached buttonholes into the first backstitch and take your needle to the back of the fabric going through the same hole as the end of the backstitch.

32. You are going to come back up through the same hole, so take your needle and thread under a small section of the cotton voile backing fabric to secure it and return up through the fabric at the beginning of the second backstitch.

33. Repeat the process for the next backstitch.

34. When you get to the third backstitch, do one detached buttonhole, one needle lace picot (the instructions for which can be found in the needle lace section of the Stitch Gallery) and one more detached buttonhole before returning to the back of the fabric to catch your thread.

35. Continue in this way working groups of three detached buttonhole stitches onto each backstitch, save for the backstitch in the centre of each scollop which has the picot as its middle stitch.

36. Thread 1 strand of *Fils Métallisé* 4024 on a size 7 embroidery needle, double it over and knot the raw ends together. Use this thread to work a small couching stitch that secures the loop of the picot to the fabric.

37. Thread 1 strand of 738 onto a size 10 bead embroidery needle, double it over and knot the raw ends together. Use this thread to bead-couch a line of beads 15°196 in the ditch between the needle lace and the satin stitch at the base of this section.

38. Fill each of these petals with weaving texture no. 4.

39. Use Dentelles 738 on a size 28 tapestry needle to do the warp threads, noted in the Stitch Gallery as shade 1.

40. Use Dentelles Ecru on a size 28 tapestry needle to do the weft threads, noted in the Stitch Gallery as shade 2.

41. Thread 1 strand of 738 onto a size 10 bead embroidery needle, double it over and knot the raw ends together. Use this thread to bead-couch a line of beads 15°196 around each petal.

Top right flower

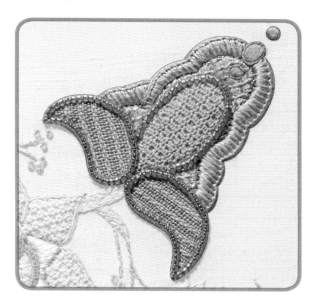

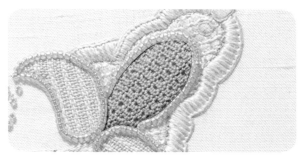

1. Fill this section in the middle of the flower with long and short stitch worked with 2 strands of 739 on a size 7 embroidery needle.

2. Using Dentelles Ecru on a size 28 tapestry needle, surround the long and short stitch with backstitch.

3. Work needle lace stitch no. 4 over the long and short stitch using the backstitch to anchor the lace stitches.

4. When you have completed everything around this area, including the bead outline of the petals below it, outline this section.

5. Thread 1 strand of 738 onto a size 10 bead embroidery needle, double it over and knot the raw ends together. Use this thread to bead-couch the outline with beads 15°196.

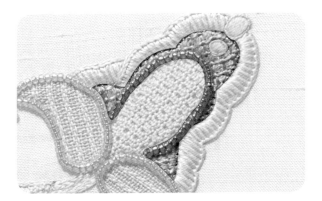

6. Using 2 strands of 712 on a size 7 embroidery needle, work vertical satin stitch over this section.

7. Take care to leave out the small circle at the top. You will come back to this later.

8. Start in the middle at the top fanning the stitches to the left and to the right as you work around each side.

9. Using 1 strand of S739 on a size 7 embroidery needle, work basic trellis couching over the satin stitch.

10. Do a small, barely visible couching stitch over each intersection.

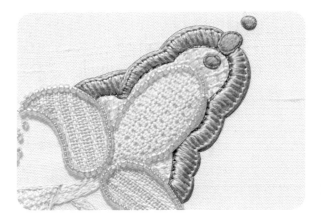

11. Fill both sections of this top edge of the flower with buttonhole stitch using 2 strands of 712 on a size 7 embroidery needle. Leave a gap between each stitch.

12. Fill in the gaps that you left with straight stitches that start at the base and end under the ridge of the buttonhole stitch. Use 1 strand of S739 on a size 7 embroidery needle.

13. Each of the circles at the top of this section is filled with padded satin stitch.

14. Use a single strand of 738 on a size 10 embroidery needle. Double it over and tie a knot at the raw end.

15. Working in a horizontal direction, do satin stitch over the circle, starting and ending the stitches just inside the lines.

16. Work a small knot on the back of your work and snip just one of the 2 strands so that what is on your needle becomes a single strand.

17. Working in a vertical direction, cover the padding with satin stitch using that single strand.

18. Using the same thread, outline the two bottom circles with small, fine stem stitch.

19. Thread 1 strand of *Fils Métallisé* 4024 on a size 7 embroidery needle, double it over and knot the raw ends together. Use this thread to work backstitch in the ditch at the base of the buttonhole stitch.

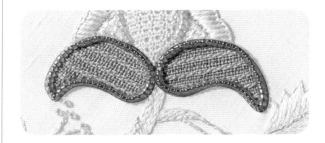

20. Fill each of the petals with weaving check and stripes no. 6.

21. Use Dentelles 738 on a size 7 embroidery needle to do the warp threads.

22. Use Dentelles Ecru for colour 1 and Dentelles 738 for colour 2, each of them threaded on a size 28 tapestry needle, to work the weft threads.

23. Thread 1 strand of 738 onto a size 10 bead embroidery needle, double it over and knot the raw ends together. Use this thread to bead-couch a line of beads 15°196 around each petal.

Middle flower

1. Fill the three petals with check and stripes no. 8.

2. Use Dentelles 738 on a size 28 tapestry needle to do the warp and weft threads, noted in the Stitch Gallery as shade 1.

3. Use Dentelles Ecru on a size 28 tapestry needle to do the warp and weft threads, noted in the Stitch Gallery as shade 2.

4. When you have completed everything around this area, outline each petal.

5. Thread 1 strand of 738 onto a size 10 bead embroidery needle, double it over and knot the raw ends together. Use this thread to bead-couch each outline with beads 15°196.

6. Using 2 strands of 712 on a size 7 embroidery needle, work vertical satin stitch over this section.

7. Using 1 strand of S739 on a size 7 embroidery needle, work basic trellis couching over the satin stitch.

8. Do a small, barely visible couching stitch over each intersection.

9. When you have completed everything around this area, outline each petal.

10. Thread 1 strand of 738 onto a size 10 bead embroidery needle, double it over and knot the raw ends together. Use this thread to bead-couch each outline with beads 15°196.

11. Pad each of the triangular shapes with horizontal satin stitch using 2 strands of 712 on a size 7 embroidery needle.

12. Cover the padding with vertical satin stitch using 1 strand of S739 on a size 7 embroidery needle.

13. When you have completed the needle lace in the petals that surround these triangles, thread 1 strand of *Fils Métallisé* 4024 on a size 7 embroidery needle, double it over and knot the raw ends together. Use this thread to work a backstitch outline around each triangle.

14. Using 1 strand of 738 doubled over on a size 10 embroidery needle, stitch a single bead at each point where the triangles meet.

15. Pad the circular shape that forms the calyx at the bottom of the flower with horizontal satin stitch using 2 strands of 712 on a size 7 embroidery needle.

16. Thread 1 strand of *Fils Métallisé* 4024 on a size 7 embroidery needle, double it over and knot the raw ends together. Use this thread to work vertical satin stitch over the padding.

17. Using 2 strands of 712 on a size 7 embroidery needle, fill each of these petals with vertical long and short stitch.

18. Using 1 strand of Dentelles Ecru on a size 28 tapestry needle, surround each petal with backstitch.

19. Using the same thread, work needle lace stitch no. 7 over the long and short stitch using the backstitch to anchor the lace stitches.

20. Still using the same thread, whip the existing backstitches on the outer edges of each petal to create the first part of the outline.

21. Using 1 strand of 738 on a size 10 embroidery needle, work a line of stem stitch around each petal on the outside of and adjacent to the whipped backstitch.

22. Thread 1 strand of *Fils Métallisé* 4024 on a size 7 embroidery needle, double it over and knot the raw ends together. Use this thread to work a small straight stitch that radiates from the tip of each petal.

Stems, tendrils and leaves

1. Fill each leaf with long and short stitch shading.

2. Start with a straight stitch at the top followed by stitches that fan around until you have reached a diagonal angle, which you stick to for the rest of each side.

3. Use 1 strand of 739 on a size 10 embroidery needle shading out to 1 strand of 712 on a size 10 embroidery needle on the edges of the leaves.

4. Using 1 strand of 738 on a size 10 embroidery needle, work an intermittent stem stitch outline around each leaf. Use the colour image as your guide.

5. Using 1 strand of 738 on a size 10 embroidery needle, work a stem stitch vein up and beyond each leaf.

6. Thread 1 strand of *Fils Métallisé* 4024 on a size 10 embroidery needle and work a line of stem stitch adjacent to the vein on the outside of the curve until the edge of the leaf.

7. Change to working on the inside of the curve adjacent to the section of the vein that extends beyond the leaf.

8. Each of the main branches is filled with rows of chain stitch worked with 1 strand of thread on a size 10 embroidery needle.

9. Use 738 for the half of the branch that is on the inside of the curve.

10. Use 739 for the half of the branch that is on the outside of the curve.

11. Outline the lighter edge with stem stitch using 1 strand of 738 thread on a size 10 embroidery needle.

12. The branch of each of these tendrils is made with whipped chain stitch.

13. Use 1 strand of 738 on a size 10 embroidery needle for the chain stitch and whip that with 1 strand of *Fils Métallisé* 4024 on a size 28 tapestry needle.

14. Thread 1 strand of 738 onto a size 10 bead embroidery needle, double it over and knot the raw ends together. Use this thread to stitch single beads 15˚196 onto the dots at the end of the branches.

The first sip

RECTANGULAR JACOBEAN PANEL

Dimensions: 260 mm (10¼") wide by 200 mm (8") high

Inspired by the colours of English bone china, the original of this design is mounted in a morning-tea tray. It can, however, be framed or used as a cushion panel. The line drawing for this design can be found at the back of the book and should be photocopied to size.

Materials

FABRIC

460 x 400 mm (18⅛ x 15¾") 200 gsm winter white
   cotton/linen blend
460 x 400 mm (18⅛ x 15¾") cotton voile backing fabric

NEEDLES

Size 7 Embroidery Needles
Size 10 Embroidery Needles
Size 26 Tapestry Needles
Size 28 Tapestry Needles
Size 10 Bead Embroidery Needles

> **STITCH INSTRUCTIONS**
> The design has been divided into sections. Each
> section is described in detail.

THREAD & BEADS

DMC STRANDED COTTON
1 skein each of

798	Dark Delft Blue
799	Medium Delft Blue
809	Delft Blue

2 skeins each of

B5200	Bright White
800	Delft Blue

DMC SATIN THREAD

S799	Medium Delft Blue
S800	Delft Blue

DMC SPECIAL DENTELLES

794	Light Cornflower Blue

DMC PERLE NO. 12

B5200	Bright White
794	Light Cornflower Blue
3753	Ultra Very Light Antique Blue

MIYUKI BEADS

15°524	2g	Sky Blue Ceylon
15°1653	2g	Dyed Semi-Matte Silver Lined Dusk Blue
11°19F	2g	Matte Silver Lined Sapphire

Top left flower

TIP

Satin threads tend to be difficult to work with because they are bouncy and inclined to fluff easily. Pull them through a thread conditioner before you use them.

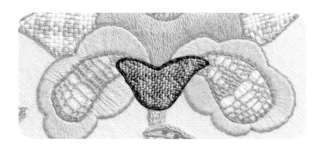

1. Fill the calyx with check and stripes no. 2 which you will find in the needle weaving section of the Stitch Gallery.

2. Use Perle no. 12 794 for shade 1 and Perle 3753 for shade 2.

3. When you have completed the embroidery in the areas surrounding the calyx, outline the needle weaving with whipped backstitch. Use 2 strands of 798 on a size 7 embroidery needle for the backstitch and whip that with 1 strand of the same thread on a size 26 tapestry needle.

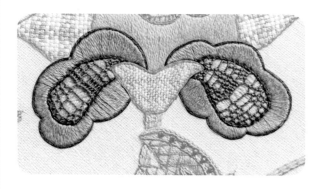

4. With 2 strands of B5200 on a size 7 embroidery needle, fill the centre of each of these side petals with long and short stitch.

5. Using 1 strand of Dentelles 794 on a size 28 tapestry needle, work fine backstitch around the edge of the stitched centre.

6. Using the same thread and starting at the tip, work needle lace stitch no. 26 over the white stitching using the backstitches to anchor the needle lace.

7. Using 2 strands of 800 on a size 7 embroidery area, work a line of split stitch on the outside line of the edge of the petal.

8. Using 1 strand of the same thread on a size 10 embroidery needle and starting at the tip of the leaf, do satin stitch to cover the border surrounding the needle laced centre.

9. Work at right angles to the split stitch, coming up immediately outside and adjacent to it.

10. Fan the stitches as you go around the shape.

11. When you have completed the embroidery in the areas surrounding these petals, outline each one with whipped backstitch. Use 2 strands of 798 on a size 7 embroidery needle for the backstitch and whip that with 1 strand of the same thread on a size 26 tapestry needle.

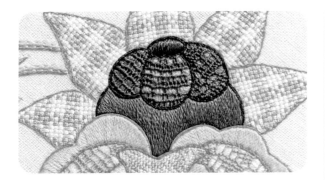

12. Fill the lower portion of this section with vertical long and short stitch shading done with 1 strand of thread on a size 10 embroidery needle.

13. Start at the base using 799 shading up to 809 in the top half of the shape.

14. When you have completed the embroidery in the areas surrounding these petals, work a whipped backstitch line down each side on the left and right edges of this section.

15. Use 2 strands of 798 on a size 7 embroidery needle for the backstitch and whip that with 1 strand of the same thread on a size 26 tapestry needle.

16. With 2 strands of B5200 on a size 7 embroidery needle, fill each of the three petals with long and short stitch.

17. Using 1 strand of Dentelles 794 on a size 28 tapestry needle, work fine backstitch around the edge of the stitched centre.

18. Using the same thread and starting at the tip, work a variation (*see below) of needle lace stitch no. 26 over the white stitching using the backstitches to anchor the needle lace.

19. Start at the tip of each petal with a tulle bar worked into each backstitch.

20. *Having whipped in the gaps back to the left side, in the next row, [work a single tulle bar each into three consecutive gaps, then miss a gap], repeating from [to] until you reach the end of the row.

21. Whip back to the left side. In the next row [work a single tulle bar into the 2 gaps between the 3 tulle bars that you worked in the previous row], repeating from [to] until you reach the end of the row.

22. After you have whipped in the gaps back to the

left side, in the next row [work a single tulle bar into the gap between the 2 tulle bars worked in the previous row], repeating from [to] until you reach the end of the row.

23. Return to the left side by whipping in the gaps and start the next sequence in the next row by working 3 tulle bars into each of the large loops in the previous row.*

24. Repeat from * to * until you have filled the petal.

25. With 2 strands of 799 (cotton) on a size 7 embroidery needle, fill the oval-shaped flower centre above the three petals with horizontal satin stitch padding.

26. Using 1 strand of S799 (satin) on a size 7 embroidery needle, cover the padding with vertical satin stitch.

27. When you have completed the embroidery in the areas surrounding these petals and their centre, outline each component with whipped backstitch. Use 2 strands of 798 on a size 7 embroidery needle for the backstitch and whip that with 1 strand of the same thread on a size 26 tapestry needle.

TIP

Satin threads can be difficult to work with because they are bouncy and inclined to fluff easily. Pull them through a thread conditioner before you use them.

28. Fill each of these petals with check and stripes no. 7.

29. Use Perle no. 12 794 for shade 1 and Perle no. 12 B5200 for shade 2.

30. Start the warp stitches in the centre of the petals using shade 1 so that, when complete, there will be a blue line down the centre.

31. When moving from one petal to the next, try to make sure that the darker lines are in line with one another.

32. Outline each petal with whipped backstitch. Use 2 strands of 798 on a size 7 embroidery needle for the backstitch and whip that with 1 strand of the same thread on a size 26 tapestry needle.

Right side flower

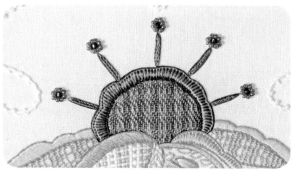

1. Fill the centre portion of this section with check and stripes no. 2 which you will find in the needle weaving section of the Stitch Gallery.

2. Use Perle no. 12 794 for shade 1 and Perle 3753 for shade 2.

3. Pad the scalloped area above the weaving with stem stitch using 2 strands of 800 on a size 7 embroidery needle.

4. With the ridge on the upper edge, cover the padding with buttonhole stitch using 2 strands of 800 on a size 7 embroidery needle. Leave a gap between each stitch.

5. Fill in the gaps that you left with straight stitches that start at the base and end under the ridge of the buttonhole stitch. Use 1 strand of S794 (satin) on a size 7 embroidery needle.

6. Work a line of whipped backstitch in the ditch between the weaving and the buttonholed border. Use 2 strands of 798 on a size 7 embroidery needle for the backstitch and whip that with 1 strand of the same thread on a size 26 tapestry needle.

7. Outline the top edge of the border with fine stem stitch done with 1 strand of 798.

8. Thread 1 strand of 800 onto a size 10 bead embroidery needle, double it over and knot the raw ends together.

9. Use this thread to stitch a bead 11°19F to the dot at the end of the stamens that radiate from the top of the flower.

10. Bring your needle up adjacent to the bead. Pick up 8 x 15°524 beads. Take the needle back through the first 3 beads to form a circle.

11. Tighten the thread, manipulating it so that the circle of beads lies around the larger bead in the middle.

12. Go down, through the fabric and thereafter come up between each bead and couch over the thread that is holding them. Take care to manipulate the beads into a neat circle as you go along.

13. Using Perle no. 12 794, stitch the stalk of each stamen with heavy chain stitch.

14. Outline one side of each stalk with fine stem stitch done with 1 strand of 798 on a size 10 embroidery needle.

15. With 2 strands of B5200 on a size 7 embroidery needle, fill the centre of each of these side petals with long and short stitch.

16. Using 1 strand of Dentelles 794 on a size 28 tapestry needle, work fine backstitch around the edge of the stitched centre.

17. Using the same thread and starting at the tip, work a variation (*see below) of needle lace stitch no. 26 over the white stitching using the backstitches to anchor the needle lace.

18. Start at the tip of each petal with a tulle bar worked into each backstitch.

19. *Having whipped in the gaps back to the left side, in the next row [work a single tulle bar each into four consecutive gaps, then miss a gap], repeating from [to] until you reach the end of the row.

20. Whip back to the left side. In the next row [work a single tulle bar into the three gaps between the four tulle bars that you worked in the previous row], repeating from [to] until you reach the end of the row.

21. Whip back to the left side. In the next row [work a single tulle bar into the two gaps between the three tulle bars that you worked in the previous row], repeating from [to] until you reach the end of the row.

22. After you have whipped in the gaps back to the left side, in the next row [work a single tulle bar into the gap between the two tulle bars worked in the previous row], repeating from [to] until you reach the end of the row.

23. Return to the left side by whipping in the gaps and start the next sequence in the next row by working 4 tulle bars into each of the large loops in the previous row.*

24. Repeat from * to * until you have filled centre of the petal.

25. Using 2 strands of 800 on a size 7 embroidery area, work a line of split stitch on the outside line of the edge of the petal.

26. Using 1 strand of the same thread on a size 10 embroidery needle and starting at the tip, do satin stitch to cover the border down each of the sides surrounding the needle laced centre.

27. Start with a straight stitch and then fan the stitches around slowly until you are working at a diagonal angle. Complete the rest of each side at that angle.

28. When you have completed the embroidery in the areas surrounding these petals, outline each one with whipped backstitch. Use 2 strands of 798 on a size 7 embroidery needle for the backstitch and whip that with 1 strand of the same thread on a size 26 tapestry needle.

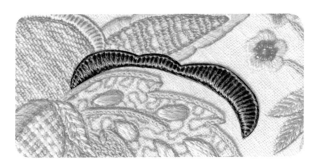

29. Pad this scraggly scalloped petal with stem stitch using 2 strands of 809 on a size 7 embroidery needle.

30. With the ridge on the upper edge, cover the padding with buttonhole stitch using 2 strands of 809 on a size 7 embroidery needle. Leave a gap between each stitch.

31. Fill in the gaps that you left with straight stitches that start at the base and end under the ridge of the buttonhole stitch. Use 1 strand of S794 (satin) on a size 7 embroidery needle.

32. Outline the top edge of the border with fine stem stitch done with 1 strand of 798 on a size 10 embroidery needle.

33. Continue the stem stitch on the bottom edge to cover the raw edges at the bottom of the buttonhole stitch.

34. Using 2 strands of 800 (cotton) on a size 7 embroidery needle, pad each of the small leaf shapes on either side of the vein in the middle of this leaf with horizontal satin stitch.

35. With a single strand of S800 (satin) on a size 7 embroidery needle, cover the padding with vertical satin stitch.

36. Using Perle no. 12 794 on a size 7 embroidery needle, stitch the vein in the centre of this leaf with heavy chain stitch.

37. Using the same thread, work heavy chain stitch around the edge of the leaf.

38. Using 2 strands of 809 on a size 7 embroidery needle and 1 strand of the same thread on a size 10 embroidery needle, fill the remaining space in this leaf with vermicelli stitch.

39. With 1 strand of 798 on a size 10 embroidery needle, outline each of the small leaf shapes and each side of the centre vein with fine stem stitch.

40. With the same thread, work fine stem stitch adjacent to the heavy chain stitch on the outside edge of the leaf. Start on the inside of the heavy chain stitch, moving to the outside when the outline changes its angle.

41. Change each time the outline alters until you finish on the other side.

42. Referring to the instructions for chain and backstitch combination in the combination stitches section of the Stitch Gallery, fill this section with vertical rows of chain stitch worked with 2 strands of 799 that are combined with backstitch worked with a single strand of S800 (satin).

43. To avoid confusing yourself, it is best to work the backstitch immediately after you have done the chain stitch and before you move onto the next row.

44. With 1 strand of 798 on a size 10 embroidery needle, outline this petal with French knots placed adjacent to the edge and at intervals of about 2 mm (¹/₁₂″).

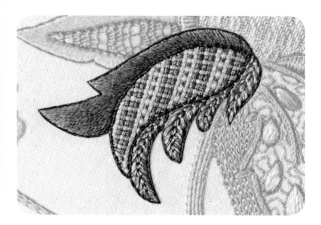

45. Fill the centre portion of this rather exotic petal with needle weaving. Use check and stripes no. 9.

46. Use Perle no. 12 794 for shade 1 and Perle no. 12 B5200 for shade 2.

47. Fill each of the four fronds on the right of the petal with fly stitch using 2 strands of 800 (cotton) on a size 7 embroidery needle.

48. When you work the stitch that holds the fly stitch, make it about 1 mm (¹/₂₄″) long. This will ensure that you have a gap of approximately the same size between the side arms of the stitches.

49. Using 2 strands of S800 (satin) on a size 7 embroidery needle, do a straight stitch in each of these gaps, hiding the end of it under the stitch in the centre.

50. Fill the portion of the petal on the left hand side with diagonal long and short stitch shading. Using 1 strand of 799 on a size 10 embroidery needle start on the inside edge, shading out to 809 in the narrow portion and through that to 800 in the wider portion at the tip of this section.

51. Using the colour image as your guide, outline each and every component of this petal with whipped backstitch. Use 2 strands of 798 on a size 7 embroidery needle for the backstitch and whip that with 1 strand of the same thread on a size 26 tapestry needle.

Small bottom flower

1. Fill the top portion of this flower with check and stripes no. 7.

2. Use Perle no. 12 794 for shade 1 and Perle no. 12 B5200 for shade 2.

3. Start the warp stitches in the centre using shade 1 so that, when complete, there will be a blue line down the centre.

4. Outline the outer edge with whipped backstitch. Use 2 strands of 798 on a size 7 embroidery needle for the backstitch and whip that with 1 strand of the same thread on a size 26 tapestry needle.

5. Using Perle no. 12 794 on a size 7 embroidery needle, stitch the stalk of each stamen with heavy chain stitch.

6. Outline one side of each stalk with fine stem stitch done with 1 strand of 798 on a size 10 embroidery needle.

7. Thread 1 strand of 798 onto a size 10 bead embroidery needle, double it over and knot the raw ends together.

8. Use this thread to stitch a bead 11°19F to the dot at the end of the stamens that radiate from the top of the flower.

9. Fill the centre portion of this section with check and stripes no. 2 which you will find in the needle weaving section of the Stitch Gallery.

10. Use Perle no. 12 794 for shade 1 and Perle 3753 for shade 2.

11. Pad the scalloped area with stem stitch using 2 strands of 809 on a size 7 embroidery needle.

12. With the ridge on the upper edge, cover the padding with buttonhole stitch using 2 strands of 809 on a size 7 embroidery needle. Leave a gap between each stitch.

13. Fill in the gaps that you left with straight stitches that start at the base and end under the ridge of the buttonhole stitch. Use 1 strand of S794 (satin) on a size 7 embroidery needle.

14. Outline the top edge of the border with fine stem stitch done with 1 strand of 798 on a size 10 embroidery needle.

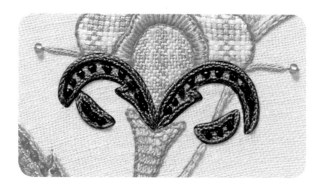

15. Outline each of these shapes with heavy chain stitch using Perle no. 12 794 on a size 7 embroidery needle.

16. Working with the leaf shapes immediately below the main part of the flower, work a line of stem stitch inside the shape immediately adjacent to and below the top line of heavy chain stitch. Use 1 strand of 798 on a size 10 embroidery needle.

17. Using the same thread, work a line of stem stitch outside the shape, immediately adjacent to and below the bottom line of heavy chain stitch.

18. Working with the crescent shapes below the flower on each side, work the stem stitch outside the shape above the top line of heavy chain stitch and inside the shape above the bottom line of heavy chain stitch.

19. Thread 1 strand of 798 onto a size 10 bead embroidery needle, double it over and knot the raw ends together.

20. Use this thread to stitch beads 15°1653 at intervals inside each of the shapes. Use the colour image as your guide.

21. With 2 strands of B5200 on a size 7 embroidery needle, pad this section with horizontal satin stitch.

22. Using the same thread, work long and short stitch over the padding.

23. Using Dentelles 794 on a size 28 tapestry needle, work fine backstitch around the entire calyx.

24. Using the same thread and starting at the tip, work needle lace stitch no. 23 over the white stitching using the backstitches to anchor the needle lace.

25. When you have completed the embroidery that surrounds the calyx, outline it with whipped backstitch. Use 2 strands of 798 on a size 7 embroidery needle for the backstitch and whip that with 1 strand of the same thread on a size 26 tapestry needle.

Forget-me-not bunches

1. Referring to the colour images, use 798 to stitch the dark forget-me-nots, 809 for the medium colour and 800 for the lightest flowers.

2. Work a line of split stitch on the perimeter line of each flower using 2 strands of the relevant thread.

3. Using 1 strand of the same thread, work satin stitch to cover the petals of each flower, starting immediately outside the split stitch and finishing on the line of the inside circle.

4. Fan the stitches as you go around.

5. Thread 1 strand of 798 onto a size 10 bead embroidery needle, double it over and knot the raw ends together.

6. Use this thread to stitch a bead 11°19F into the centre of the flower.

7. Bring your needle up adjacent to that bead.

8. Pick up 8 x 15°1653 beads.

9. Take the needle back through the first 3 beads to form a circle.

10. Tighten the thread, manipulating it so that the circle of beads lies around the larger bead in the middle.

11. Go down, through the fabric and thereafter come up between each bead and couch over the thread that is holding them. Take care to manipulate the beads into a neat circle as you go along.

12. Using Perle no. 12 794 on a size 7 embroidery needle, stitch the stalk of each flower with heavy chain stitch.

13. Outline one side of each stalk with fine stem stitch done with 1 strand of 798 on a size 10 embroidery needle.

14. Thread 1 strand each of 800, 809 and 799 onto a size 7 embroidery needle.

15. Using this thread combination, fill the circle at the base of the leaves with a layer of French knots.

16. Work a second layer, over the first, in the middle two thirds of the circle, allowing each knot to lie gently on the knots below it.

17. Thread 1 strand of 798 onto a size 10 bead embroidery needle, double it over and knot the raw ends together.

18. Use this thread to stitch between 5 and 11 beads 15°1653 at intervals between the French knots.

19. The number of beads will depend on the size of the circle, as each one of the three is a different size.

20. Referring to the colour images, use 798 to stitch the dark leaves, 809 for the medium colour and 800 for the lightest leaves.

21. Fill each leaf with fly stitch using 2 strands of the relevant thread on a size 7 embroidery needle.

22. Start at the tip with a straight stitch and make the leg of each fly stitch long enough for a small gap to form on the sides of the stitches.

23. Fill these gaps with straight stitches that start on the side and finish under the vein created by the fly stitch. Use 2 strands of Satin S800 on a size 7 embroidery needle.

24. Outline one side of each leaf with fine stem stitch using 1 strand of 798 on a size 10 embroidery needle.

Branches and leaves

1. There are three of these leaves in this design and each one is done in the same way.

2. Fill the main body of the leaf with long and short stitch shading starting closest to the vein with 799, shading out to 809 on the edge and, where there is space at the end of the tips on the left of each leaf, to 800.

3. In each case, use 1 strand of thread on a size 10 embroidery needle.

4. Using 1 strand of 798 on a size 10 embroidery needle, work basic trellis couching over the long and short stitch shading.

5. Outline the outside edge of the leaf with whipped backstitch.

6. Use 2 strands of 798 on a size 7 embroidery needle for the backstitch and whip that with 1 strand of the same thread on a size 26 tapestry needle.

7. Using Perle no. 12 794 on a size 7 embroidery needle, work a line of heavy chain stitch on the double lines at the top of the leaf and the double lines that make up the vein.

8. Work a line of stem stitch inside and immediately adjacent to both of the heavy chain stitch lines at the top of the leaf. Use 1 strand of 788 on a size 10 embroidery needle.

9. Using the same thread, work a line of stem stitch outside and immediately adjacent to both of the heavy chain stitch lines that make up the vein of the leaf.

10. Thread 1 strand of 798 onto a size 10 bead embroidery needle, double it over and knot the raw ends together.

11. Use this thread to stitch beads 15°1653 at intervals inside each set of double lines.

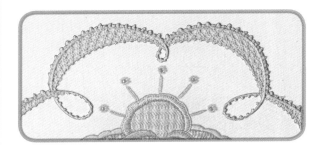

The lace edge

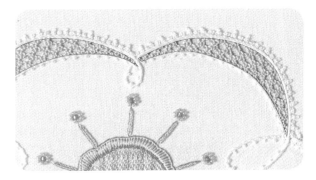

12. All of the main branches in the design are worked in the same way using 2 strands of 800 on a size 7 embroidery needle.

13. Starting on the edge that is on the inside of the curve of the branch, work a line of chain stitch.

14. Finish off at the other end.

15. Going back to the beginning, work a second line of chain stitch, also finishing off at the other end.

16. With two strands of 799 on a size 26 tapestry needle, whip the adjoining side of the chain stitch together.

17. Continue with a third line of chain stitch, which starts at the beginning and ends at the end.

18. Whip the adjoining side of the second and third row together.

19. Where the stems start with a narrow area and widen out, you may have a portion of that stem filled with only one row of chain stitch. When you whip that, start by whipping only one side of the chain stitch up to where the second line of chain stitch starts.

20. When you get to the start of the second line of chain stitch, incorporate the adjoining side into the whipping and continue to the end.

21. With 1 strand of 798 on a size 10 embroidery needle, outline the inside curve of each branch with a row of fine stem stitch. Use the colour images as guide.

1. With 1 strand of perle no. 12 B5200 on a size 7 embroidery needle, outline each of the crescent shapes that form the lace edge of the design with backstitch.

2. Using the same thread on a size 26 tapestry needle and starting on the inside, longest edge, fill these shapes with needle lace stitch no. 8 using the back-stitch to anchor the needle lace.

3. Follow each shape, decreasing the length of the needle lace rows as necessary.

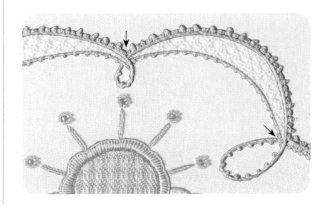

4. The nature of needle lace, when used as an embroidery technique, is that the edge is rough and messy. It always needs to be outlined somehow and that outline should not be done on the outside but, rather, worked within the very edge of the needle lace so that you are, in effect, working to cover the original backstitch.

5. Starting on the outside edge of the needle lace, at the beginning of the crescent, as indicated by the left arrow, work a line of whipped chain stitch along that edge, around the loop, finishing at the point indicated by the right arrow.

6. You should use 3 strands of B5200 on a size 7 embroidery needle for the chain stitch and whip that with 2 strands of the same thread on a size 26 tapestry needle.

7. Now outline the inside edge of the needle lace using 2 strands of B5200 on a size 7 embroidery needle for the chain stitch and whip that with 1 strand of the same thread on a size 26 tapestry needle.

8. With 2 strands of B5200 on a size 7 embroidery needle, work intermittent French knots against the whipped chain stitch on the inside edge, continuing on the inside of the loops that face inwards between the lace crescents.

9. Using Perle no. 12 B5200 on a size 7 embroidery needle, work an odd number of backstitches immediately adjacent to the whipped chain stitch, on the outside edge of each lace crescent. Each of the stitches should be long enough to accommodate 3 detached buttonhole stitches.

10. Working with the same thread on a size 26 tapestry needle, starting at the beginning of a crescent and coming up in the same hole as the backstitch, work 3 detached buttonhole stitches into the first backstitch.

11. Go into the fabric in the same hole as the end of that backstitch.

12. Miss the next backstitch.

13. Come up in the same hole at the beginning of the following backstitch and do 3 detached buttonhole stitches, going into the fabric in the same hole as the end of that backstitch.

14. Continue in this way, working on every alternate backstitch, until you reach the end of the crescent. If you have an odd number of backstitches, as instructed, you should do the last group of detached buttonhole stitches on the last available backstitch.

15. Working with the same thread on the same needle, you now need to fill in the missed backstitches.

16. Come up in the same hole as the first available backstitch.

17. Work one detached buttonhole stitch into that backstitch, followed by a needle lace picot, instructions for which are in the needle lace section of the Stitch Gallery. Work another detached buttonhole into the same backstitch and go into the fabric in the same hole as the end of that backstitch.

18. Work all of the missed backstitches in this way to provide the frilly edge reminiscent of the crocheted edge that would be found on a tray cloth.

Vyesna Prishla

RECTANGULAR JACOBEAN CLOCK FACE

Dimensions: 170 mm (6¾") wide by 116 mm (4½") high

Inspired by the simple, yet remarkably effective shapes of Russian art, much of it reminiscent of the shapes used in Jacobean embroidery, the original of this design has been specifically designed for the Sudberry House Petite Mantel Clock. This clock can be purchased online and website links appear in the Buyer's Guide at the back of this book. The line drawing for this design can be found at the back of the book and should be photocopied to size.

Materials

FABRIC

360 x 360 mm (14⅓ x 14⅓") 200 gsm winter white
   cotton/linen blend
360 x 360 mm (14⅓ x 14⅓") cotton voile backing fabric

NEEDLES

Size 7 Embroidery Needles
Size 10 Embroidery Needles
Size 10 Bead Embroidery Needles
Size 26 Tapestry Needles

THREAD & BEADS

DMC STRANDED COTTON

152	Medium Light Shell Pink
221	Very Dark Shell Pink
223	Light Shell Pink
224	Very Light Shell Pink
225	Ultra Very Light Shell Pink
322	Dark Baby Blue
334	Medium Baby Blue
561	Very Dark Celadon Green
562	Medium Jade
563	Light Jade
564	Very Light Jade
676	Very Light Old Gold
3722	Medium Shell Pink
3828	Hazelnut Brown
3829	Very Dark Old Gold
3847	Dark Teal Green
3848	Medium Teal Green
3849	Light Teal Green
3866	Ultra Very Light Mocha Brown

DMC METALLIC THREAD

E301	Copper
E436	Golden Oak
E677	White Gold
E3849	Aquamarine Blue

MIYUKI BEADS

15°198	2g	Copper Lined Opal
15°1424	2g	Dyed Silver Lined Teal
15°1883	2g	Transparent Wine Gold Lustre

STITCH INSTRUCTIONS

The design consists of two flowers, the mirror image of which is opposite the first in each instance. The instructions have been divided into two sections. Each section is described in detail.

The two larger flowers

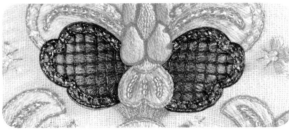

7. Using the same threads, work a row of whipped backstitch on the outer line of the petal.

8. Thread 1 long strand of 3866 on a size 10 bead embroidery needle. Double it over and tie the raw ends together with a knot.

9. Use this thread to stitch beads 15°1883 at intervals between the two lines of dull gold whipped backstitch.

10. When you have completed the surrounding areas and using 1 strand of 221 on a size 10 embroidery needle, do a row of fine stem stitch adjacent to and outside the outer dull gold line of whipped backstitch to outline and define each of these petals.

1. Fill each of these petals with long and short stitch shading.

2. Start at the base of the petal using 1 strand 3722 on a size 10 embroidery needle, shading through 223 and 152 to 224 at the tip.

3. With 1 strand of 221 on a size 10 embroidery needle, work basic trellis couching over the long and short stitch shading, using the colour image as your guide.

4. Do a small couching stitch at each intersection using the same thread.

5. Outline the shaded area with backstitch worked adjacent to the edge of the previous stitching. Use 2 strands of E436 on a size 7 embroidery needle.

6. Whip the backstitch with 1 strand of the same thread on a size 26 tapestry needle.

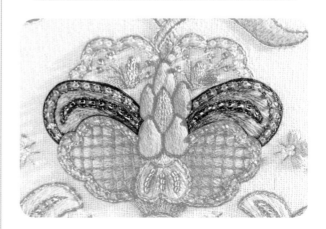

11. Outline each side of the middle vein with whipped backstitch using 1 strand of E301 on a size 7 embroidery needle.

12. Thread 1 long strand of 3866 on a size 10 bead embroidery needle. Double it over and tie the raw ends together with a knot.

13. Use this thread to stitch beads 15°1424 at intervals between the two lines of copper coloured whipped backstitch.

14. Fill each of these petals with long and short stitch shading.

15. Start at the base of the petal using 1 strand 223 on a size 10 embroidery needle, shading through 152 and 224 to 225 at the tip.

16. Outline the shaded area with whipped backstitch worked adjacent to the edge of the previous stitching. Use 1 strand of E677 on a size 7 embroidery needle.

17. Using the same thread, work a row of whipped backstitch on the outer line of the petal.

18. Thread 1 long strand of 3866 on a size 10 bead embroidery needle. Double it over and tie the raw ends together with a knot.

19. Use this thread to stitch beads 15°198 at intervals between the two lines of white gold whipped backstitch.

20. When you have completed the surrounding areas and using 1 strand of 221 on a size 10 embroidery needle, do a row of fine stem stitch adjacent to and outside the outer white gold line of whipped backstitch to outline and define each of these petals.

TIP

When working satin stitch with metallic thread you need to tighten your tension to a point past your comfort level because it is inclined to loosen and look untidy.

21. Using 2 strands of 3849 stranded cotton on a size 7 embroidery needle, pad each of the small leaves with horizontal satin stitch.

22. Cover the padding with vertical satin stitch using E3849 metallic thread on a size 7 embroidery needle.

23. Using 1 strand of E436 on a size 7 embroidery needle, work small stem stitches on each of the small stems that radiate from the metallic teal leaves.

24. Thread 1 long strand of 3866 on a size 10 bead embroidery needle. Double it over and tie the raw ends together with a knot.

25. Use this thread to stitch beads 15°1883 at the tip of each stem.

26. Using 1 strand of E677 on a size 7 embroidery needle, do a row of whipped backstitch on each of the lines that form the outer edge of this petal.

27. With 1 strand of 224 on a size 10 embroidery needle, work a line of fine stem stitch immediately above and adjacent to the inner white gold line.

28. With 1 strand of 225 on a size 10 embroidery needle, work a line of fine stem stitch immediately above and adjacent to the previous line of stem stitch.

29. With 1 strand of 221 on a size 10 embroidery needle, work a line of fine stem stitch immediately above and adjacent to the outer white gold line.

30. With 1 strand of 224 on a size 10 embroidery needle, work a line of fine stem stitch immediately above and adjacent to the previous line of stem stitch.

31. Thread 1 long strand of 3866 on a size 10 bead embroidery needle. Double it over and tie the raw ends together with a knot.

32. Use this thread to stitch beads 15°198 at intervals between the 2 lines of white gold whipped backstitch.

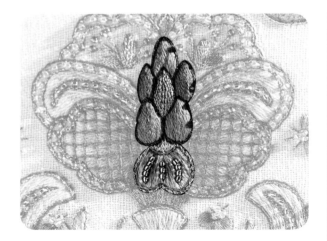

33. Pad each of the teardrop shapes with horizontal satin using 2 strands of cotton on a size 7 needle.

34. Use 3849 for the pair in the bottom row and the single shape at the tip. Use 3848 for the 3 in the middle row.

35. Changing to 1 strand of thread on a size 10 embroidery needle, cover the padding with vertical satin stitch.

36. Starting at the bottom, use 3849 for the 2 in that row.

37. Moving to the middle row, use 3848 for the 2 shapes on the sides and metallic E3849 for the shape in the middle.

38. Use 3849 for the shape at the tip.

39. When you have completed the embroidery in the areas surrounding these shapes, outline each of them individually with fine stem stitch. Use 1 strand of 3847 on a size 10 embroidery needle.

40. With 2 strands of 676 on a size 7 embroidery needle, pad the small gold circle with horizontal satin stitch.

41. Cover the padding with vertical satin stitch using 1 strand of E677 on a size 7 embroidery needle.

42. Fill the golden petal shape below that circle with long and short stitch shading using 1 strand of thread on a size 10 embroidery needle.

43. Start at the base with 676 shading to 3828 at the tip.

44. Thread 1 long strand of 3847 on a size 10 bead embroidery needle. Double it over and tie the raw ends together with a knot.

45. Use this thread to bead-couch between 3 and 5 beads 15°1424 in 3 lines over the golden shading. Use the colour image as your guide.

46. When you have completed the embroidery in the surrounding areas, outline the petal shape with back-stitch using 1 strand of E677 on a size 7 embroidery needle.

47. Whip the backstitch with 1 strand of the same thread.

48. With 1 strand of 3829 on a size 10 embroidery needle, work a line of fine stem stitch on the inside of and adjacent to the white gold whipped backstitch.

49. Using the same thread, outline the small white gold circle with a line of fine stem stitch.

50. Using the colour image as your guide, fill each of the green leaves at the tip of the larger flower with long and short stitch shading.

51. Start on the lower side of each leaf with 1 strand of 563 on a size 10 embroidery needle, shading up to 564 on the upper side.

52. When you have completed the embroidery in the surrounding areas, outline each leaf with backstitch using 1 strand of E677 on a size 7 embroidery needle.

53. Whip the backstitch with 1 strand of the same thread.

54. Working between the metallic thread outline and the shading, do a line of fine stem stitch along the bottom edge using 1 strand of 561 on a size 10 embroidery needle.

55. Working between the metallic thread outline and the shading, do a line of fine stem stitch along the top edge using 1 strand of 562 on a size 10 embroidery needle.

56. Fill each of the blue flowers with padded satin stitch, using 2 strands of thread on a size 7 embroidery needle for the horizontal padding and 1 strand on a size 10 embroidery needle for the vertical satin stitch.

57. Use 322 for the tallest flower and 334 for the shorter bloom to the left of it.

58. Thread 1 long strand of 3866 on a size 10 bead embroidery needle. Double it over and tie the raw ends together with a knot.

59. Use this thread to stitch 3 beads 15°198 into the small circle that forms the centre at the top of each flower.

60. Using 1 strand of E301 on a size 7 embroidery needle, work the stems of the flowers in whipped backstitch.

61. Using the same thread, work 3 straight stitches on the lines that radiate out of the top of each flower.

62. Each of the small green leaves is a detached chain stitch.

63. Work with 2 strands of thread on a size 7 embroidery needle, using 562 for the darker leaves towards the base of the stem and 563 for the lighter leaves closer to the top.

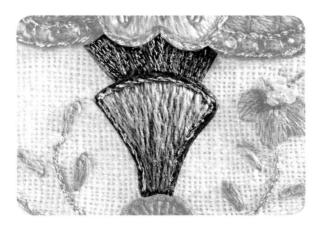

64. Thread 2 strands of E301 onto a size 7 embroidery needle. Thread up another size 7 embroidery needle with strands of 561.

65. Using the thread on these needles alternately, start in the middle of the upper portion highlighted in the image, with 2 straight stitches using the E301.

66. Follow this with 2 straight stitches using 561.

67. Keep going in this way until you reach the edge, finishing off with 2 green stitches.

68. Return to the middle and complete the other side in the same way.

69. Moving to the lower portion, fill this area with long and short stitch shading using 1 strand of thread on a size 10 embroidery needle.

70. Start at the base with 562, shading through 563 to 564 at the tip.

71. Outline the left, top and right sides of the shape with whipped backstitch using 1 strand of E677.

72. Work a line of fine stem stitch adjacent to the outside of the white gold whipped backstitch using 1 strand of 561 on a size 10 embroidery needle.

Following the instructions above, embroider the second larger flower in the same way.

The two smaller flowers

1. Outline each side of the middle vein with whipped backstitch using 1 strand of E301 on a size 7 embroidery needle.

2. Thread 1 long strand of 3866 on a size 10 bead embroidery needle. Double it over and tie the raw ends together with a knot.

3. Use this thread to stitch beads 15°1424 at intervals between the two lines of copper coloured whipped backstitch.

4. Fill each of these petals with long and short stitch shading.

5. Start at the base of the petal using 1 strand 223 on a size 10 embroidery needle, shading through 152 and 224 to 225 at the tip.

6. Outline the shaded area with whipped backstitch worked adjacent to the edge of the previous stitching. Use 1 strand of E436 on a size 7 embroidery needle.

7. When you have completed the surrounding areas and using 1 strand of 221 on a size 10 embroidery needle, do a row of fine stem stitch adjacent to and outside the outer dull gold line of whipped backstitch to outline and define each of these petals.

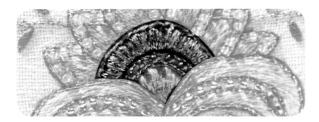

8. Pad the golden yellow wedge shape in the bottom half of this section with horizontal satin stitch using 2 strands of 676 on a size 7 embroidery needle.

9. Cover the padding with long and short stitch shading using 1 strand of thread on a size 10 embroidery needle.

10. Start at the base with 3828 shading to 676 at the tip.

11. Using 2 strands of 3849 on a size 7 embroidery needle, pad between the lines of the semi-circular portion at the top of this section.

12. Starting on the left, and using the same thread, do buttonhole stitch over the padding. The ridge of

the button-hole stitch should face the top and you should leave a small gap between each of the stitches.

13. With 2 strands of E3849 (metallic) on a size 7 embroidery needle, work straight stitches in the gaps that you left between the buttonhole stitches. Start at the base and bury the end of the stitch under the ridge of the buttonhole stitch.

14. Using 1 strand of E677 on a size 7 embroidery needle, work a line of whipped backstitch adjacent to the bottom edge of the buttonhole stitch semi-circle and another line adjacent to the top edge of the golden yellow shaded area.

15. Thread 1 long strand of 3866 on a size 10 bead embroidery needle. Double it over and tie the raw ends together with a knot.

16. Use this thread to stitch beads 15°1883 at intervals between the two lines of white gold whipped backstitch.

17. Using 1 strand of 3847 on a size 10 embroidery needle, do a line of fine stem stitch in the ditch between the base of the teal-coloured semi-circle of buttonhole stitch and the top line of white gold whipped backstitch.

18. When you have completed the petals above this area of the design, using the same thread, work a line of fine stem stitch on the outside of and adjacent to the ridge of the buttonhole stitched semi-circle.

19. Each petal that radiates out of the top of this flower is stitched in the same way.

20. Using 1 strand of thread on a size 10 needle, fill the centre of each petal with long and short stitch shading.

21. Working from the base, start with 224 shading up to 152 at the tip.

22. Using 1 strand of E677 on a size 7 embroidery needle, work a line of whipped backstitch on each of the double lines that form the outer edge of these petals.

23. Thread 1 long strand of 3866 on a size 10 bead embroidery needle. Double it over and tie the raw ends together with a knot.

24. Use this thread to stitch beads 15°198 at intervals between the two lines of white gold whipped backstitch.

25. When you have completed all of the petals and using 1 strand of 221 on a size 10 embroidery needle, do a row of fine stem stitch adjacent to and outside the outer white gold line of whipped backstitch to outline and define each of these petals.

26. Fill each of the blue flowers with padded satin stitch, using 2 strands of thread on a size 7 embroidery needle for the horizontal padding and 1 strand on a size 10 embroidery needle for the vertical satin stitch.

27. Use 322 for the flowers that come out of the stem area and 334 for the blooms that come out of either side of the flower.

28. Thread 1 long strand of 3866 on a size 10 bead embroidery needle. Double it over and tie the raw ends together with a knot.

29. Use this thread to stitch 3 beads 15°198 into the small circle that forms the centre at the top of each flower.

30. Using 1 strand of E301 on a size 7 embroidery needle, work the stems of the flowers in whipped backstitch.

31. Using the same thread, work 3 straight stitches on the lines that radiate out of the top of each flower.

32. Each of the small green leaves is a detached chain stitch.

33. Work with 2 strands of thread on a size 7 embroidery needle, using 562 for the darker leaves towards the base of the stem and 563 for the lighter leaves closer to the top.

34. Using the colour image as your guide, fill each of the green leaves with long and short stitch shading.

35. Start at the base of each leaf with 1 strand of 563 on a size 10 embroidery needle, shading up to 564 at the tip.

36. When you have completed the embroidery in the surrounding areas, outline each leaf with backstitch using 1 strand of E677 on a size 7 embroidery needle.

37. Whip the backstitch with 1 strand of the same thread.

38. Working between the metallic thread outline and the shading, do a line of fine stem stitch along the bottom edge using 1 strand of 561 on a size 10 embroidery needle.

39. Working between the metallic thread outline and the shading, do a line of fine stem stitch along the top edge using 1 strand of 562.

Late harvest

RECTANGULAR JACOBEAN PANEL

Dimensions: 365 mm (14½") wide by 115 mm (4½") high

Inspired by the colours of a South African autumn sunset, the original of this design is mounted in a drinks' tray. The line drawing for this design can be found at the back of the book and should be photocopied to size.

Materials

FABRIC

550 x 320 mm (21¾ x 12½") cotton/linen natural
  coloured fabric
550 x 320 mm (21¾ x 12½") cotton voile backing fabric

ADDITIONAL HABERDASHERY

250 x 250 mm (10 x 10") khaki green poly cotton fabric
5 metres (3½ yards) copper stumpwork wire
Clear fray-stop

NEEDLES

Size 7 Embroidery Needle
Size 26 Tapestry Needle
Size 10 Embroidery Needle
Size 10 Bead Embroidery Needle
Size 22 Chenille Needle
Size 18 Chenille Needle
Size 12 Quilter's Needle
Size 5 Milliner's Needle

THREAD & BEADS

DMC STRANDED COTTON

436	Tan
437	Light Tan
451	Dark Shell Grey
452	Medium Shell Grey
453	Light Shell Grey
738	Very Light Tan
778	Very Light Antique Mauve
779	Dark Cocoa
950	Light Desert Sand
3011	Dark Khaki Green
3012	Medium Khaki Green
3013	Light Khaki Green
3782	Light Mocha Brown
3787	Dark Brown Grey
3857	Dark Rosewood
3858	Medium Rosewood

MIYUKI BEADS

15°13F	4g	Matte Silver Lined Dark Smokey Amethyst
15°336	4g	Wine Lined Peridot Luster
15°1421	4g	Silver Lined Golden Olive
15°1631	2g	Semi-Matte Silver Lined Saffron
15°2422F	2g	Matte Silver Lined Topaz
5°131R	2g	Crystal AB
8°256	1	Purple Lined Amethyst AB

SWAROVSKI 40SS 2028 FLAT BACK RHINESTONES

001GSHA	x 38	8.5 mm Golden Shadow

STITCH INSTRUCTIONS

The design is divided into sections. Each section is described in detail.

Central fruit and surrounds

1. Fill the middle of the fruit with battlement couching using 2 strands of each thread on size 7 embroidery needles.

2. Work the first layer using 779, spacing the lines of the trellis about 6 mm (¼") apart.

3. Follow this shade with 451, then 452 and finally 453.

4. Thread 1 long strand of 779 on a size 10 bead embroidery needle. Double it over and tie the raw ends together with a knot.

5. Coming up at the base of each available space between the four trellis lines, pick up a 15°2422F bead.

6. Complete the stitch by going into the fabric just above the lightest trellis lines thereby couching that intersection.

7. Whilst a portion of each side of the fruit in the colour image on this page is hidden by the stumpwork leaves that are ultimately attached at the top of the fruit, the lines of the main drawing are not masked.

8. Fill the space between the lines, on both sides, with stem stitch padding using 2 strands of 3858 on a size 7 embroidery needle.

9. Using the same thread, with the ridge forming on the outside edge, cover the padding with buttonhole stitch. Leave a gap approximately the width of a straight stitch between each stitch.

10. Fill the gaps between the buttonhole stitches with straight stitches using 2 strands of 778 on a size 7 embroidery needle.

11. Using 1 strand of 3857 on a size 10 embroidery needle, work a fine outline of stem stitch on the outside edge adjacent to the ridge, on each side.

12. Using 2 strands of the same thread on a size 7 embroidery needle, work a line of stem stitch in the ditch between the buttonhole stitch and the battlement couching, covering the raw edges of the buttonhole stitch on each side.

13. Fill each of the 5 leaves at the base of this fruit with long and short stitch shading.

14. Using 1 strand of thread on a size 10 embroidery needle and working from base to tip, start with 451, shading through 452 up to 3013 at the tip.

15. Outline each leaf with fine stem stitch using 1 strand of 3013 on a size 10 embroidery needle.

16. Thread 1 long strand of 779 on a size 10 bead embroidery needle. Double it over and tie the raw ends together with a knot.

17. Pick an 8°256 and a 15°13F bead.

18. Return down through the larger bead and pull the thread through thereby securing it into place with the smaller bead.

19. Bring the needle through the fabric on the edge of the buttonhole stitch above and adjacent to the large bead.

20. Pick up 7 x 15°13F beads and go back into the fabric on the opposite side, pulling through so that the small beads form a semi-circle around the bottom of the large bead.

21. Couch over the thread between each of the small beads to hold the circle in place.

22. Fill each of the leaves that radiate from the top of the fruit with woven trellis, outlined with beaded palestrina stitch.

23. Following the guidelines in the table below, use 2 strands of thread for each of the shades in the woven trellis.

24. Use a size 7 embroidery needle for shades 1 and 2.

25. Use a size 26 tapestry needle for shades 3 and 4.

26. Use a single strand on a size 10 bead embroidery needle, doubled over and knotted, for the beaded palestrina stitch.

TIP

If you vary the lines between the trellis stitches in the woven trellis couching, each variation can look like it was done with a different technique.

27. Working from the left use the threads and beads listed below:

	Shade 1	Shade 2	Shade 3	Shade 4	Outline
Left Leaf	3858	950	3012	3012	15°336 with 3857
Middle Leaf	3011	452	452	3013	15°1631 with 3011
Right Leaf	3011	452	452	3013	15°1631 with 3011

34. The three large leaves in this section are done in the same way.

35. Using a single strand of 3011 on a size 10 bead embroidery needle, double it over and knot the raw ends together.

36. Starting at the tip of the leaf and following the lines drawn for the vein, stitch a line of between 3 and 5 x 15°1421 beads onto each diagonal line, taking the thread through the bead lines at least twice to make sure that each line doesn't move out of place.

37. When you reach the base of the leaf, using the same thread, work your way to the tip again by doing a long straight stitch between each line of beads to accentuate the green.

38. At the base of each leaf, the final bead line is longer. These beads should be attached as a continuous line with bead-couching.

39. Fill the leaves with diagonal long and short stitch shading which starts vertical at the top and fans around to a 45 degree angle.

40. Using 1 strand on a size 10 embroidery needle, in each instance, start adjacent to the vein with 778 for the larger, right hand leaf at the top and the one

28. Fill this autumn leaf with diagonal long and short stitch shading that starts vertical at the top and fans around to a 45 degree angle.

29. Using 1 strand on a size 10 embroidery needle, in each instance, start adjacent to the vein with 436.

30. Working outwards, shade through 3012 to 3858 on the outer edge.

31. Outline the outer edge with fine stem stitch using 1 strand of 3857 on a size 10 embroidery needle.

32. Thread a single strand of 3857 on a size 10 bead embroidery needle, double it over and knot the raw ends together.

33. With this bead-couch a line of 15°336 beads up the vein, continuing the line to the end of the tendril that continues out of the leaf.

on the lower right side of the fruit. Start the upper left leaf with 452.

41. Working outwards, shade through 738 to 3012 on the outer edge of all three of the leaves.

42. Outline the outer edges with fine stem stitch using 1 strand of 3011 on a size 10 embroidery needle.

43. Using a single strand of 738 on a size 12 quilter's needle, double it over and knot the raw ends together.

44. Following the instructions for covering a large bead with thread in the bead embroidery section of the Stitch Gallery, place a 5°131R bead in the centre of the small purple flower, covering it with the thread on your small needle and placing a 15°2422F bead in the middle on the last stitch.

45. Pad each petal of the small flower with horizontal satin stitch using 2 strands of 452.

46. Work vertical long and short stitch over the padding with 1 strand of thread on a size 10 embroidery needle. Start at the base with 451 shading up to 452 on the tip.

47. Using a single strand of 3011 on a size 10 bead embroidery needle, double it over and knot the raw ends together.

48. Start at the tip of each small leaf with a straight stitch, continuing with beaded fly stitch using a 15°1421 bead to the base.

49. Using 2 strands of 3012 on a size 7 embroidery needle, do a straight stitch in the gaps between the fly stitches, burying the end of the stitch under the bead.

50. Following the instructions in the twisted stitches section of the Stitch Gallery, do the stems of the flower and all the highlighted tendrils with twisted couching using 3787.

Wired items

> **TIP**
>
> The wired stumpwork leaves will be attached to your work at the very end, once you have finished everything else and washed your piece. Trace all of the templates onto the khaki green fabric. The instructions for the leaves are given in the section that is relevant to each set.

- Trace the stumpwork shapes on pages 158-159 onto the khaki green lightweight fabric using either a pencil or a blue tailor's pen.
- Arrange them in sections so that you know which set is which, trying to fit them into an area that will fit into an 8 inch hoop.
- Place the fabric in the hoop, making sure that it is pulled tight and stays taut.

> **TIP**
>
> Use a plastic hoop so that if you want to wash these wired items (you should wash them, it will bring them to life), you will be able to run them under a tap, soap them, rinse them and hang them up to dry without taking them out of the hoop.

- First work the embroidery and bead stitching as described for each set of leaves.
- When you have completed the embroidery, measure and cut the suggested length of copper wire for each leaf.
- Fold the wire in half and pinch the fold with a pair of pliers.
- Open it slightly and place the pinched fold adjacent to and on the outer edge of the embroidery at the tip of the leaf.
- Working with one strand of the suggested thread, start with a few backstitches slightly below the tip of the leaf (sorry, no knots on this one, they will show when you cut your leaves out).
- Work a row of about 5 fine overcasting stitches around the tip.
- This is sufficient to hold the wire onto the fabric. You do not want to couch the remainder of the wire into place because the couching stitches will become mixed up with your overcasting stitches. When you later unpick them, there will be gaps left by the stitches that are removed.
- Thereafter, working down one side of the leaf, attach the wire with overcasting stitches, keeping it very close to the edge of the embroidery, bending the wire to follow the shape as you go along.
- Come up on the outside from underneath the wire, with the needle facing outwards at an angle.

- Take the thread over the wire and go back into the fabric on the inside, with the needle facing inwards at an angle.
- When you reach the bottom of the leaf, end off the thread with a few backstitches that are formed within the body of the leaf, but not showing on the top side of the embroidery.
- Return to the tip and work the remaining side, stitching the wire adjacent to the outside edge in the same way.
- When you reach the base of the leaf, lay the two tails side by side and place two or three stitches over both tails to keep them together. End the thread in the same way as before.
- When you have completed all of the wired items, you will probably want to wash them, as suggested above.
- When they are completely dry, squeeze a continuous line of fray-check onto the fabric outside the covered wire, allowing it to bleed onto no more than just the covered wire.

TIP

Test the rate of flow by squeezing some fraycheck onto another section of the fabric before working on the real thing.

TIP

The angle of the needle is very important, because you should have no stray stitches on the outside that might potentially be snipped when you cut your leaf out.

- Once the fray-check has dried, use a small, really sharp pair of scissors to cut the leaves away from the fabric.
- Angle your scissors outwards, as if you are coming up and out from underneath. Cut as smoothly as you can, doing longer cuts rather than short snips. After you have made sure that each leaf is perfectly cut, with no stray threads sticking out, snip the two tails to equal lengths.
- Choose the spot where you wish to place your leaf and drive a size 18 chenille needle through the fabric to the point where the eye of the needle is in the fabric.
- This creates a channel for your tails to be pushed through the fabric. And you should do just that.
- Once the wire is through the fabric, fold it back and stitch it to the back of the embroidery with two strands of 3782 on a size 7 embroidery needle.
- Leaving a small tail at the end of the stitching, snip off the superfluous wire and fold the small tail back so that it prevents the wire from slipping out of the stitching.

51. Having traced the template for the centre fruit leaves onto a piece of lightweight khaki green fabric, fill each of them with diagonal long and short stitch shading that starts vertical at the top and fans around to a 45 degree angle.

52. Using 1 strand on a size 10 embroidery needle, in each instance, start adjacent to the vein with 3012.

53. Working outwards, shade through 3013 and 950 to 3858 on the outer edge, using the colour image as your guide.

54. Bead-couch a line of 15°336 beads along the length of the vein using 1 strand of 3857 on a size 10 bead embroidery needle.

55. Measure and cut 2 x 150 mm (6") and 1 x 80 mm (3½") pieces of wire.

56. Following the instructions for wired items on the preceding pages, stitch the wire adjacent to the edge of the long and short stitch shading with 1 strand of 3857 on a size 10 embroidery needle.

57. When you have completed all of the embroidery in this project, attach the leaves as indicated in the colour image, according to the instructions for wired items.

Moving on to the right of the central fruit, the instructions are in groups that have been divided as conveniently as possible for the sake of the instructions:

Right side large bunch of grapes and surrounds

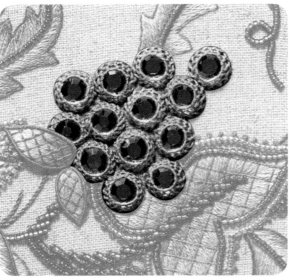

1. Each grape is a Swarovski flat back crystal, as listed in the material requirements at the start of these instructions.

2. Hold the flat back crystal in place on the circle drawn for its placement. Each circle has been drawn slightly smaller than the actual size of the crystal so that the lines do not show.

3. Use a waste thread that is a completely different colour from the thread you will use to stitch the golden tan cage that holds the flat back crystal in place.

4. Come through the fabric at the top of the crystal. Go into the fabric at the bottom thus forming a straight stitch that goes down the mid-line of the crystal.

5. Now work three more stitches to form a star that holds the crystal in place. The first should go over the horizontal mid-line.

6. The last two go from top right to bottom left and then from top left to bottom right. When working the last two stitches, whip under the intersection of the first two stitches. This holds them all together and stops them from sliding off the crystal.

7. Finish off by coming up one more time and doing a knot over the intersection. This will make it easy to pull these stitches out.

8. Using 2 strands of either 436 or 437 on a size 7 embroidery needle, do a line of backstitch around and adjacent to the crystal. Using the colour images as your guide, stitch some with the lighter thread and some with the darker.

TIP

Try to avoid snagging the waste stitches that hold the crystal in place, but don't be too obsessive about it. It is sometimes difficult to avoid.

9. Using the same thread, continue by working a detached buttonhole stitch under each backstitch.

10. When you get back around to the first buttonhole stitch, take your needle through the loop of that

stitch to secure the end of the row and continue in the opposite direction working a detached buttonhole stitch into each of the loops created in the first row.

11. Work a third row in the same way.

12. When you reach the end of that row, continue in the same direction, whipping through each of the loops.

13. When you get back to where you started the whipping stitches, pull the thread to tighten the last row and to make sure that it fits snugly against the crystal.

14. Ease the needle under detached buttonhole stitches and take it through the fabric to end off. Don't pull the thread too tightly, as this will create a kink in the last row of the cage you have created.

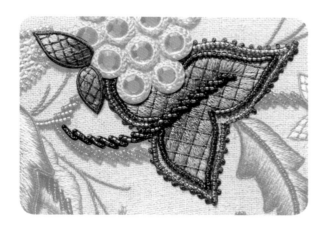

15. Fill the main body of this leaf with diagonal long and short stitch shading that starts vertical at the top and fans around to a 45 degree angle and eventually to a 90 degree angle at the base of the leaf.

16. Using 1 strand on a size 10 embroidery needle, in each instance, start adjacent to the vein with 3012.

17. Working outwards, shade through 3013 and 778 on the outer edge, and 950 at the tips. Use the colour image as your guide.

18. Using 1 strand of 3011 on a size 10 embroidery needle, work basic trellis couching over the long and short stitch shading.

19. Using a single strand of 3011 on a size 10 bead embroidery needle, double it over and knot the raw ends together.

20. Starting at the tip of the leaf and following the lines drawn for the vein, stitch a line of between 3 and 5 x 15°1421 beads onto each diagonal line, taking the thread through the bead lines at least twice to make sure that each line doesn't move out of place.

21. When you reach the base of the stem, using the same thread, work your way to the tip again by doing a long straight stitch between each line of beads to accentuate the green.

22. Still using 3011 on a bead embroidery needle, bead-couch a line of 15°1421 beads onto the inside line that runs around the perimeter of the leaf.

23. Changing your thread to 3013 on the beading needle, bead-couch a line of 15°1631 beads onto the outside line that runs around the perimeter of the leaf.

24. Using 2 strands of 3011 on a size 7 embroidery needle, work French knots adjacent to the outside line of beads. Leave a small gap between the knots.

25. Referring to the instructions for the wired items, fill 1 x large and 1 x small 'small grape bunch leaves' with long and short stitch shading. Use 1 strand of thread on a size 10 embroidery needle, start at the base of the leaf with 3012, shading through 3013 and 778 to 950.

26. With 1 strand of 3011 on a size 10 embroidery needle, work basic trellis couching over the long and short stitch shading.

27. Cut and measure 2 x 40 mm (1½") pieces of wire and stitch them on with 1 strand of 3011 on a size 10 embroidery needle.

28. Attach these leaves at the end of the project, placing them approximately between the second and third grapes.

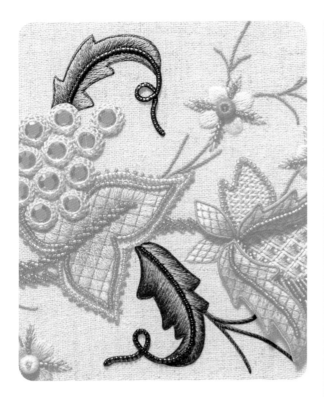

29. These leaves are worked in the same way as the autumn leaf that extends from the centre fruit.

30. Starting with the leaf that extends from the large grape leaf, using 1 strand on a size 10 embroidery needle, in each instance, start adjacent to the vein with 436.

31. Working outwards, shade through 3012 to 3858 on the outer edge.

32. Outline the outer edge with fine stem stitch using 1 strand of 3857 on a size 10 embroidery needle.

33. Thread a single strand of 3857 on a size 10 bead embroidery needle, double it over and knot the raw ends together.

34. With this bead-couch a line of 15°336 beads up the vein, continuing the line to the end of the tendril that continues out of the leaf.

35. The leaf that comes out of the grapes uses 451 shading out to 452 and 3013 for the long and short stitch.

36. The stem stitch outline is worked with 3011 and the bead vein is done with 15°13F stitched on with 779.

37. The bead stems which, in the first instance, go into the bunch of grapes and, in the second, go towards the far left fruit, are done in the same way.

38. Thread a single strand of 779 on a size 10 bead embroidery needle, double it over and knot the raw ends together.

39. Bearing in mind that in the colour image part of the stem is hidden by a stumpwork leaf, start adjacent to the top of the bunch of grapes, following the lines drawn for that stem. Stitch a line of between 1 and 5 x 15°13F beads onto each diagonal line, taking the thread through the bead lines at least twice to make sure that each line doesn't move out of place.

40. At the base of the stem, the final bead line is longer. These beads should be attached as a continuous line with bead-couching.

41. When you reach the base of the stem, using the same thread, work your way to the tip again by doing a long straight stitch between each line of beads to accentuate the violet.

42. The second stem that leads to the far right fruit is done in the same way using 15°336 beads and 3857.

43. Using a single strand of 779 on a size 12 quilter's needle, double it over and knot the raw ends together.

44. Following the instructions for covering a large bead with thread in the bead embroidery section of the Stitch Gallery, place a 5°131R bead in the centre of the small purple flower, covering it with the thread on your small needle and placing a 15°13F bead in the middle on the last stitch.

45. Pad each petal of the small flower with horizontal satin stitch using 2 strands of 778.

46. Work vertical long and short stitch over the padding with 1 strand of thread on a size 10 embroidery needle. Start at the base with 778 shading up to 738 on the tip.

47. Using a single strand of 3011 on a size 10 bead embroidery needle, double it over and knot the raw ends together.

48. Start at the tip of each small leaf with a straight stitch, continuing with beaded fly stitch using a 15°1421 bead to the base.

49. Using 2 strands of 3012 on a size 7 embroidery needle, do a straight stitch in the gaps between the fly stitches, burying the end of the stitch under the bead.

50. Following the instructions in the twisted stitches section of the Stitch Gallery, do the stems of the flower and all the highlighted tendrils with twisted couching using 3787.

Far right fruits and surrounds

1. Fill the middle of the fruit with battlement couching using 2 strands of each thread on a size 7 embroidery needle.

2. Work the first layer using 3858 spacing the lines of the trellis about 6 mm (¼") apart.

3. Follow this shade with 3013, then 778 and finally 950.

4. Thread 1 long strand of 3012 on a size 10 bead embroidery needle. Double it over and tie the raw ends together with a knot.

5. Coming up at the base of each available space between the four trellis lines, pick up a 15°1631 bead.

6. Complete the stitch by going into the fabric just above the lightest trellis lines thereby couching that intersection.

7. Whilst a portion of each side of the fruit in the colour image on this page is hidden by the stumpwork leaves that are ultimately attached at the top of the fruit, the lines of the main drawing are not masked.

8. Fill the space between the lines, on both sides, with stem stitch padding using 2 strands of 451 on a size 7 embroidery needle. You will cover the bead lines and should, therefore, refer to them on the line drawing at the back of the book to determine the angles you will need to follow.

9. Thread 1 long strand of 779 on a size 10 bead embroidery needle. Double it over and tie the raw ends together with a knot.

10. Thread 2 strands of 451 on a size 5 milliner's needle.

11. Start at the bottom centre, working from the inside to the outside. Using the bead embroidery needle, pick up 8 x 15°13F beads, lay them over the padding, going through the fabric on the other side. Go through the beads a second time for stability.

12. Using the milliner's needle, working from the inside to the outside, work a bullion knot over the padding.

13. Follow this with a line of beads and continue alternating beads and bullions until you have covered the padding up to the top of the fruit. Adjust the length of both the bead lines and bullions as necessary.

14. Return to the bottom centre and do the same on the other side.

15. Fill the small leaf that extends from the top of the fruit on the left with long and short stitch shading.

16. Use 1 strand of thread on a size 10 embroidery needle, start at the base of the leaf with 3012, shading through 3013 and 452 to 950.

17. With 1 strand of 3011 on a size 10 embroidery needle, work basic trellis couching over the long and short stitch shading.

18. Outline the leaf with fine stem stitch using the same thread.

19. Fill the leaf on the right with woven trellis outlined with beaded palestrina stitch.

20. Following the guidelines in the table below, use 2 strands of thread for each of the shades in the woven trellis.

21. Use a size 7 embroidery needle for shades 1 and 2 and a size 26 tapestry needle for shades 3 and 4.

22. Use a single strand on a size 10 bead embroidery needle, doubled over and knotted, for the beaded palestrina stitch.

23. Use the following threads and beads:

Shade 1	Shade 2	Shade 3	Shade 4	Outline
3012	452	3013	3013	15°1631 with 3011

24. The two large leaves in this section are done in the same way as the leaves that come out of the central fruit.

25. Using a single strand of 3011 on a size 10 bead embroidery needle and between 2 and 5 x 15°1421 beads for the vein.

26. When you reach the base of the leaf, using the same thread, work your way to the tip again by doing a long straight stitch between each line of beads to accentuate the green.

27. Using 1 strand on a size 10 embroidery needle, in each instance, start adjacent to the vein with 778 for the larger leaf on the left of the fruit. Start the smaller, right side leaf with 452.

28. Working outwards, shade through 738 to 3012 on the outer edge of both of the leaves.

29. Outline the outer edges with fine stem stitch using 1 strand of 3011 on a size 10 embroidery needle.

30. Using a single strand of 738 on a size 12 quilter's needle, double it over and knot the raw ends together.

31. Following the instructions for covering a large bead with thread in the bead embroidery section of the Stitch Gallery, place a 5°131R bead in the centre of

the small purple flower, covering it with the thread on your small needle and placing a 15°2422F bead in the middle on the last stitch.

32. Pad each petal of the small flower with horizontal satin stitch using 2 strands of 3858.

33. Work vertical long and short stitch over the padding with 1 strand of thread on a size 10 embroidery needle. Start at the base with 3858 shading up to 436 on the tip.

34. Using a single strand of 3011 on a size 10 bead embroidery needle, double it over and knot the raw ends together.

35. Start at the tip of each small leaf with a straight stitch, continuing with beaded fly stitch using a 15°1421 bead to the base.

36. Using 2 strands of 3012 on a size 7 embroidery needle, do a straight stitch in the gaps between the fly stitches, burying the end of the stitch under the bead.

37. Following the instructions in the twisted stitches section of the Stitch Gallery, do the stems of the flower and all the highlighted tendrils with twisted couching using 3787.

38. Using 436 and 437, attach the flat back crystals with a buttonhole stitch cage as instructed previously.

39. The small leaf that extends out of the top is filled with long and short stitch shading.

40. Use 1 strand of thread on a size 10 embroidery needle, start at the base of the leaf with 3012, shading through 3013 and 778 to 950.

41. With 1 strand of 3011 on a size 10 embroidery needle, work basic trellis couching over the long and short stitch shading.

42. Using the same thread, outline the leaf with fine stem stitch.

43. Referring to the instructions for the large bunch of grapes work the stem in the same way using 15°13F beads and 779.

44. The small stumpwork leaves are worked in the same way as you have done for the large bunch of grapes.

45. Work the autumn leaf in the same way as the ones you have already done using 436, shading through 3012 to 3858 to the edge. Outline with 3857 and use the same thread to bead-couch the 15°336 beads that form the vein and tendril.

46. Following the instructions for wired items, trace the template for the far right fruit leaves onto a piece of lightweight khaki green fabric.

47. Fill the two side leaves with diagonal long and short stitch shading that starts vertical at the top and fans around to a 45 degree angle.

48. Using 1 strand on a size 10 embroidery needle, in each instance, start adjacent to the vein with 451.

49. Working outwards, shade through 452 to 3013 on the outer edge, using the colour image as your guide.

50. With a single strand of 3011 on a size 10 embroidery needle, work basic trellis couching over the entire leaf.

51. Bead-couch a line of 15°13F beads along the length of the vein using 1 strand of 779 doubled over on a size 10 bead embroidery needle.

52. Measure and cut 2 x 150 mm (6") pieces of wire. Attach them, as instructed, with a single strand of 3011 on a size 10 embroidery needle.

53. Fill the small leaf with vertical long and short stitch shading, starting at the base with 1 strand of 3012 on a size 10 embroidery needle. Shade through 3013 and 452 to 950 at the tip.

54. With a single strand of 3011 on a size 10 embroidery needle, work basic trellis couching over the entire leaf.

55. Measure and cut a 6 cm (2½") piece of wire and attach it, as instructed, with a single strand of 3011 on a size 10 embroidery needle.

56. Attach the leaves at the end of the project following the instructions for wired items.

Moving on to the left of the central fruit, the instructions are in groups that have been divided as conveniently as possible for the sake of the instructions:

Centre left grapes and surrounds

1. Using 436 and 437 to create the buttonhole stitch bead cages, attach the Swarovski flat back crystals as previously instructed.

2. Take note that the stumpwork leaves for the larger of these two bunches of grapes appear separately in the stumpwork templates.

3. Apart from that fact, work both leaves embroidered onto the fabric and the small stumpwork leaves as instructed for the small bunch of grapes attached to the far right fruit.

4. The beaded stems that run into both bunches of grapes are worked in the same way as previous grape stems using bead 15°13F.

5. The autumn leaves which extend from the larger bunch of grapes are worked in the same way as previous autumn leaves.

6. Use 451 shading through 452 to 453 for the violet leaf, outlining with 3013. The vein extending into the tendril uses 15°13F beads, bead-couched with 779.

7. The autumn leaf at the bottom uses 436 shading through 3012 to 3858 and is outlined with 3857. The vein extending into the tendril uses 15°336 beads, bead-couched with 3857.

8. The remaining leaves are worked in the same way as the others that have been described, using 15° 1421 beads and 3011 for the vein.

9. The lower leaf uses 778 shading through 738 to 3012 whilst the upper leaf uses 451 shading through 738 to 3012. Both leaves are outlined with 3011.

10. The small flowers are worked in the same way as those previously described.

11. The purple flower at the bottom uses 738 to cover the large bead, with a small bead 15°2422F in the dent. The padding of the petals is done with 452 and the long and short shading starts at the base with 451 shading up to 452.

12. The small flower at the top uses 738 to cover the large bead, with a small bead 15°2422F in the dent.

13. The padding of the petals is done with 3858 and the long and short shading starts at the base with 3858 shading up to 436.

14. The beaded fly stitch leaves for both flowers use beads 15°1421 with 3011 for the fly stitch and 3013 for the straight stitches in between.

15. As before, the small tendrils and stems are twisted couching done with 3787.

Left top flower and surrounds

1. Fill the semi-circle at the top of the flower with stem stitch padding using 2 strands of 3858 on a size 7 embroidery needle.

2. Cover the padding with long and short stitch shading working from base to tip with 1 strand of 3857 on a size 10 embroidery needle shading up to 3858.

3. Pad the section below with stem stitch using 2 strands of 738 on a size 7 embroidery needle.

4. Cover the padding with alternating lines of beads and bullion knots referring to the original line drawing to set the angles.

5. Use beads 15°2422F stitched on with 1 strand of 437 folded double on a size 10 bead embroidery needle.

6. Start in the centre with a line of 5 beads, going through the beads twice so that they remain stable.

7. Follow the line of beads with a bullion knot worked with 2 strands of 738 on a milliner's needle.

8. Keep going in this way until you reach the end of the first side, reducing the lengths of the bead lines and the bullions as necessary and finishing with a bullion knot.

9. Return to the middle and complete the other side in the same way.

10. Using a double strand of 437 on a size 7 embroidery needle, work a straight stitch on either side of each bead line.

11. Changing to 1 strand of the same thread on a size 10 embroidery needle outline the outer edges of the last bullion knot on either side with fine stem stitch.

12. Work the section below in the same way using 778 for the padding and the bullion knots and 3857 for the bead lines, straight stitches and stem stitch outlines. Use beads 15°336.

13. Fill the tubular section of the flower with woven trellis outlined on the two long sides with bead-couching.

14. Use a size 7 embroidery needle for shades 1 and 2 and a size 26 tapestry needle for shades 3 and 4.

15. Use a single strand on a size 10 bead embroidery needle, doubled over and knotted, for the bead-couching.

16. Use the following threads and beads:

Shade 1	Shade 2	Shade 3	Shade 4	Outline
452	950	3013	3013	15°1631 with 3013

17. The petals at the bottom of the flower are a combination of 3 stitched directly onto the fabric and 2 stumpwork petals. All are filled with long and short stitch shading using the same threads.

18. Start at the base with 1 strand of 3012 on a size 10 embroidery needle, shading through 3013 and 738 to 3858 at the tip.

19. Outline the petals that you have stitched directly onto the project with fine stem stitch using 1 strand of 3857.

20. Measure and cut a 6 cm (2½") piece of wire and attach it, as instructed, with a single strand of 3857 on a size 10 embroidery needle.

21. Attach the leaves at the end of the project following the instructions for wired items.

22. Starting within the large bunch of grapes, work the bead stem as you have all previous stems using bead 15°336 and thread 3857.

23. Work the autumn leaf that extends from the right of the flower as you have all other similar leaves using the 436, 3012, 3858 and 3857 combination of threads and beads 15°336.

24. Work the small bunch of grapes as you have all other similar grapes using 436 and 437 for the Swarovski flat back buttonhole stitch cages, the 3011, 3012, 3013, 778 and 950 combination of threads for the leaves, and the 779 and bead 15°13F combination for the stem.

25. Work all tendrils with twisted couching using 3787.

Far left fruit and surrounds

1. Fill the middle of the fruit with battlement couching using 2 strands of each thread on a size 7 embroidery needle.

2. Work the first layer using 3012, spacing the lines of the trellis about 6 mm (¼") apart.

3. Follow this shade with 436, then 778 and finally 950.

4. Thread 1 long strand of 3857 on a size 10 bead embroidery needle. Double it over and tie the raw ends together with a knot.

5. Coming up at the base of each available space between the four trellis lines, pick up a 15°336 bead.

6. Complete the stitch by going into the fabric just above the lightest trellis lines, thereby couching that intersection.

7. Whilst a portion of each side of the fruit in the colour image on this page is hidden by the stumpwork leaves that are ultimately attached at the top of the fruit, the lines of the main drawing are not masked.

8. Fill the space between the lines, on both sides, with stem stitch padding using 2 strands of 451 on a size 7 embroidery needle. You will cover the bead lines and should, therefore, refer to them on the line drawing at the back of the book to determine the angles you will need to follow.

9. Thread 1 long strand of 779 on a size 10 bead embroidery needle. Double it over and tie the raw ends together with a knot.

10. Thread 2 strands of 451 on a size 5 milliner's needle.

11. Start at the bottom centre, working from the inside to the outside. Using the bead embroidery needle, pick up 8 x 15°13F beads, lay them over the padding, going through the fabric on the other side. Go through the beads a second time for stability.

12. Using the milliner's needle, working from the inside to the outside, work a bullion knot over the padding.

13. Follow this with a line of beads and continue alternating beads and bullions until you have covered the padding up to the top of the fruit. Adjust the length of both the bead lines and bullions as necessary.

14. Return to the bottom centre and do the same on the other side.

15. Work the bead stem as you have all previous stems using bead 15°336 and thread 3857.

16. Work the autumn leaf that extends from the right of the flower as you have all other similar leaves using the 436, 3012, 3858 and 3857 combination of threads and beads 15°336.

17. Work all tendrils with twisted couching using 3787.

18. Moving to the leaf which extends from the top of the fruit on the right, fill this with long and short stitch shading.

19. Using 1 strand of thread on a size 10 embroidery needle, start at the base with 779, shading through 451 and 738 to 3013 at the tip.

20. With 1 strand of 3011 on a size 10 embroidery needle, work basic trellis couching over the long and short stitch shading.

21. Outline the leaf with fine stem stitch using the same thread.

22. Following the instructions for wired items, trace the template for the far right fruit leaves onto a piece of lightweight khaki green fabric.

23. Fill the two side leaves with diagonal long and short stitch shading that starts vertical at the top and fans around to a 45 degree angle.

24. Using 1 strand on a size 10 embroidery needle, in each instance, start adjacent to the vein with 451.

25. Working outwards, shade through 738 to 3012 on the outer edge, using the colour image as your guide.

26. Bead-couch a line of 15°13F beads along the length of the vein using 1 strand of 779 doubled over on a size 10 bead embroidery needle.

27. Measure and cut 2 x 150 mm (6") pieces of wire. Attach them, as instructed, with a single strand of 3011 on a size 10 embroidery needle.

28. Fill the small stumpwork leaves with vertical long and short stitch shading, starting at the base with 1 strand of 779 on a size 10 embroidery needle. Shade through 451 and 738 to 3012 at the tip.

29. With a single strand of 3011 on a size 10 embroidery needle, work basic trellis couching over the shading.

30. Measure and cut 2 x 6 cm (2½") pieces of wire and attach them, as instructed, with a single strand of 3011 on a size 10 embroidery needle to the leaves.

31. Attach the leaves at the end of the project following the instructions for wired items.

Inflorescence

RECTANGULAR JACOBEAN PANEL

Dimensions: 110 mm (4⅓") high by 211 mm (8⅓") wide

The original of this design has been stitched into a small needle book. It can, however, be made into a handbag or used as a cushion panel. The line drawing for this design can be found at the back of the book and should be photocopied to size.

Materials

FABRIC

400 x 400 mm (15¾" x 15¾") hunter's green taffeta
400 x 400 mm (15¾" x 15¾") cotton voile backing fabric

ADDITIONAL HABERDASHERY

100 x 50 mm (4 x 2") felt
100 x 50 mm (4 x 2") applique magic

NEEDLES

Size 7 Embroidery Needles
Size 26 Tapestry Needles
Size 10 Embroidery Needles
Size 10 Bead Embroidery Needles
Size 22 Chenille Needles

THREAD & BEADS

DMC STRANDED COTTON

0155	Blue Violet
0333	Very Dark Blue Violet
0340	Medium Blue Violet
0469	Avocado Green
0712	Cream
0738	Very Light Tan
0739	Ultra Very Light Tan
0772	Very Light Green
0798	Dark Delft Blue
0799	Medium Delft Blue
0800	Pale Delft Blue
0839	Dark Beige Brown
3022	Medium Brown Grey
3023	Light Brown Grey
3607	Light Plum
3609	Ultra Light Plum

KOEKSISTER THREAD

02	Oak
06	Royal Purple
07	Light Green Emerald

DMC *FILS MÉTALLISÉ*

4052	Light Green Emerald
4012	Ultra Violet
4018	Pink Amethyst
4038	Blue Sapphire

DMC METALLIC

E898	Dark Oak

MIYUKI BEADS

#1.0026	2g	Silver Lined Olive
#1.0353	2g	Cobalt Lined Sapphire AB
15°0132FR	2g	Matte Transparent Light Topaz AB
15°0143FR	2g	Matte Transparent Chartreuse AB
15°0177	2g	Transparent Cobalt AB
15°0197	2g	Copper Lined Crystal
15°0209	2g	Fuchsia Lined Crystal
15°1427	2g	Dyed Silver Lined Dark Violet
15°1527	2g	Sparkle Celery Lined Crystal
15°2442	2g	Crystal Ivory Gold Luster

SWAROVSKI 34SS 2028 FLAT BACK RHINESTONES

502	x 5	7.2 mm Fuchsia

STITCH INSTRUCTIONS
The design is divided into sections. Each section
is described in detail.

Crystal buds

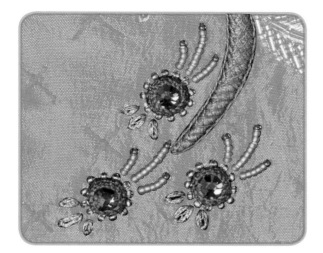

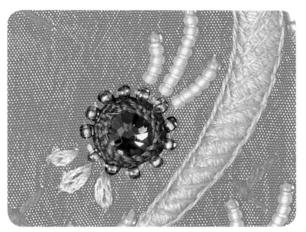

1. Hold the flat back crystal in place on the circle drawn for its placement.

2. Use a waste thread that is a completely different colour from the thread you will use to stitch the pink cage that holds the flat back crystal in place.

3. Come through the fabric at the top of the crystal. Go into the fabric at the bottom thus forming a straight stitch that goes down the mid-line of the crystal.

4. Now work three more stitches to form a star that holds the crystal in place. The first should go over the horizontal mid-line.

5. The last two go from top right to bottom left and then from top left to bottom right. When working the last two stitches, whip under the intersection of the first two stitches. This holds them all together and stops them from sliding off the crystal.

6. Finish off by coming up one more time and doing a knot over the intersection. This will make it easy to pull these stitches out.

7. Using 2 strands of 3607 on a size 7 embroidery needle, do a line of backstitch around and adjacent to the crystal.

TIP

Try to avoid snagging the waste stitches that hold the crystal in place, but don't be too obsessive about it. It is sometimes difficult to avoid.

8. Using the same thread, continue by working a detached buttonhole stitch under each backstitch.

9. When you get back around to the first buttonhole stitch, take your needle through the loop of that stitch to secure the end of the row and continue in the opposite direction working a detached buttonhole stitch into each of the loops created in the first row.

10. Work a third row in the same way.

11. When you reach the end of that row, continue in the same direction, whipping through each of the loops.

12. When you get back to where you started the whipping stitches, pull the thread to tighten the last row and to make sure that it fits snugly against the crystal.

13. Ease the needle under detached buttonhole stitches and take it through the fabric to end off. Don't pull the thread too tightly as this will create a kink in the last row of the cage you have created.

14. Thread one strand of 712 onto a size 10 embroidery needle. Double it over and tie the two ends together with a knot. Using this thread stitch beads 15°2442 adjacent to the thread cage holding the crystal into place. Leave a small gap between each bead and take care to space them evenly apart.

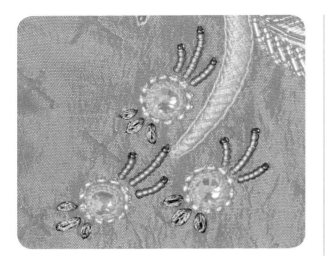

15. Thread one strand of 738 onto a size 10 bead embroidery needle. Double it over and tie the two ends together with a knot. Using this thread, attach the beads that form the three stamens of each flower with bead-couching.

16. Use between four and nine 15°132FR beads for the main stem of the stamen with a single 15°209 bead for the tip.

17. Each of the leaves radiating out of the flower is a detached chain stitch done with koeksister thread 07 on a size 22 chenille needle. For a description of how to make koeksister thread, refer to the Threads And Their Needles section of the Materials chapter at the beginning of the book.

TIP

When using Koeksister thread, make sure that all of the threads in the chain go through the fabric evenly and that no loops remain on the top. If necessary, manipulate the thread with a spare needle.

Main flower

1. Thread one strand of 469 onto a size 10 bead embroidery needle. Double it over and tie the two ends together with a knot. Using this thread, bead-couch a row of beads onto each diagonal line that makes up the wide outer border of the petal. Come up on the outside edge. Pick up between 1 to 3 x 15°143FR, 1 x #1.26 bugle and 1 x 15°1527 bead. Vary the number of each of the beads according to the length of the line.

2. With 1 strand of *Fils Métallisé* 4052 on a size 7 embroidery needle, do a long straight stitch between the bead lines to create a slight sparkle.

3. Starting at the tip, with a straight stitch, fill the inside of each leaf with diagonal satin stitches. On each side, the stitches should start at the end of the bead lines and finish on the line which forms the vein running up the middle of the leaf. Use 2 strands of 3607 on a size 7 embroidery needle.

4. Thread one strand of *Fils Métallisé* 4018 onto a size 7 embroidery needle. Double it over and tie the two ends together with a knot. Using this thread, work a line of stem stitch up the vein.

5. Each of these petals is worked in the same way.

6. Starting at the base and working towards the tip, fill each of the petals with long and short stitch using koeksister thread 06 on a size 22 chenille needle.

7. Using 1 strand of 333 on a size 10 embroidery needle, do basic trellis couching over the long and short stitch.

8. Couch a bead 15°1427 over each intersection.

9. Using *Fils Métallisé* 4012 on a size 7 embroidery needle, outline each petal with stem stitch.

10. Work each of these petals in the same way.

11. Starting at the base with 1 strand of 333 and working towards the tip, fill each of the petals with long and short stitch. Shade through 155 to 340.

12. In the case of the two petals with pink towards the tip, shade though to 3609.

13. Use 772 for the petal with green towards the tip.

14. In all instances shade through to 712 at the tip.

15. Using the colour image as your guide and using *Fils Métallisé* 4012 on a size 7 embroidery needle, work basic trellis couching to cover approximately half of each petal.

16. With the same thread, work a small couching stitch over each intersection.

17. Using *Fils Métallisé* 4012 on a size 7 embroidery needle, outline each petal with stem stitch.

TIP

Lubricate *Fils Métallisé* thread with a thread conditioner to minimise shredding and make the thread easier to work with.

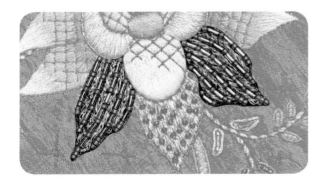

18. Thread one strand of 469 onto a size 10 bead embroidery needle. Double it over and tie the two ends together with a knot.

19. Using this thread and starting at the base with a 15°143FR bead followed by a #1.26 bugle bead, bead-couch a row of beads on each line, alternating the beads and finishing with as many of the round beads as you need to complete it.

20. Using koeksister thread 06 on a size 22 chenille needle, fill in the spaces between the bead lines with chain stitch.

21. Whip the chain stitch with 2 strands of 155 on a size 26 tapestry needle.

22. Using *Fils Métallisé* 4052 on a size 7 embroidery needle, outline each petal with stem stitch.

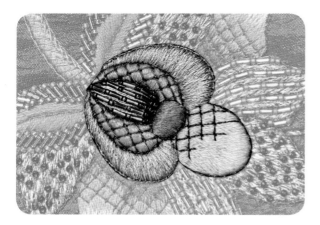

23. Trace each of the shapes of the templates on page 157 onto the paper side of applique magic.

24. Press the applique magic onto the felt with a hot iron.

25. Using the tracing on the applique magic as your guide, cut out the template shapes with a pair of sharp scissors.

26. Peel the paper off each of the felt shapes. The flossy applique magic should remain on what is now the back of your felt shapes.

27. With the applique magic facing down, tack the largest of the templates onto the centre of the flower.

28. With the applique magic facing down, tack the smaller shapes, which form the blue centre of this section, into place over the existing felt thereby creating a double layer.

29. Press the felt with a hot iron to secure it into place. You will undo the tacking stitches as you work each section.

TIP

The taffeta on which you are working scorches easily so use a pressing cloth when working with a hot iron.

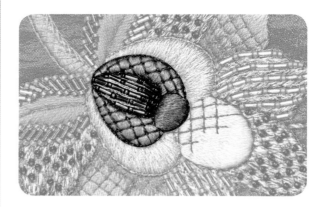

30. Using 1 strand of 799 on a size 10 embroidery needle, do vertical satin stitch over the oval shape at the tip of this section.

31. Using 1 strand of 800 on a size 10 embroidery needle, do horizontal satin stitch over the shapes on the two sides. Fan the stitching around the shape.

32. Using 1 strand of 798 on a size 7 embroidery needle, work basic trellis couching to cover each of the side shapes. With the same thread, work a small couching stitch over each intersection.

33. Thread one strand of 798 onto a size 10 bead embroidery needle. Double it over and tie the two ends together with a knot.

34. Using this thread and starting at the base with a 15°177 bead followed by a #1.353 bugle bead, bead-couch a line of beads up the centre of the space remaining in the centre, alternating the beads and finishing with as many of the round beads as you need to reach the tip.

35. Work two similar lines on either side of the central bead line, using as many beads as you require and taking care to space them so that they cover the central space.

36. Using koeksister thread 07 on a size 22 chenille needle, work a long straight stitch between the lines of beads, coming up at the base and going in at the tip.

37. When you have completed the areas surrounding these shapes, thread one strand of *Fils Métallisé* 4038 onto a size 7 embroidery needle. Double it over and tie the two ends together with a knot. Using this thread, work outlines of stem stitch all the way around each of the shapes.

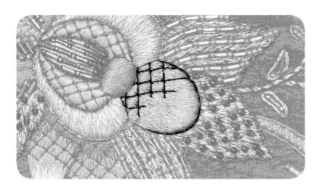

38. Cover the single layer of felt in this area with long and short stitch shading.

39. Start at the base with 1 strand of 738 on a size 10 embroidery needle, shading through 739 to 712 at the tip.

40. Using 1 strand of E898 on a size 7 embroidery needle, work basic trellis couching to cover the bottom half of the shape. With the same thread, work a small couching stitch over each intersection.

41. When you have stitched and outlined the two green sections below this shape, outline the outer edge of this section with stem stitch using 1 strand of E898 on a size 7 embroidery needle.

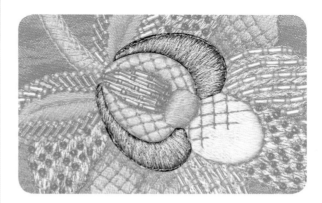

42. Using 1 strand of koeksister thread 07 on a size 22 chenille needle, do horizontal satin stitch over the shapes on the two sides. Fan the stitching around the shape.

43. Thread one strand of *Fils Métallisé* 4052 onto a size 7 embroidery needle. Double it over and tie the two ends together with a knot. Using this thread, work outlines of stem stitch on the outer edge of each of the shapes.

Bud branches and small leaves

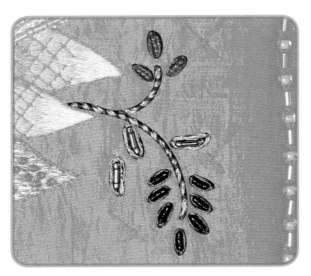

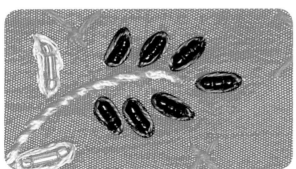

1. Thread 1 strand of 155 onto a size 10 bead embroidery needle. Double it over and tie the two ends together with a knot. Using this thread, bead-couch 3 x 15°1427 beads onto each of the lines of the buds.
2. Using 2 strands of 155 on a size 7 embroidery needle, work a detached chain stitch around the line of beads to complete the bud.

3. Thread 1 strand of 3607 onto a size 10 bead embroidery needle. Double it over and tie the two ends together with a knot. Using this thread, bead-couch 3 x 15°209 beads onto each of the lines of the buds.
4. Using 2 strands of 3607 on a size 7 embroidery needle, work a detached chain stitch around the line of beads to complete the bud.

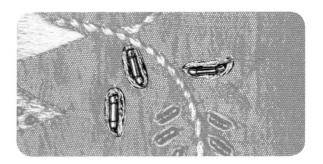

5. Thread 1 strand of 469 onto a size 10 bead embroidery needle. Double it over and tie the two ends together with a knot. Using this thread, bead-couch 1 x 15°197, 1 x #1.26 bugle and 1 x 15°197 bead onto each of the lines for the leaves.
6. Using 1 strand of koeksister thread 07 on a size 22 chenille needle, work a detached chain stitch around the line of beads to complete the leaves.

7. Using 1 strand of koeksister thread 02 on a size 22 chenille needle, work the stems with chain stitch.
8. Whip the chain stitch with two strands of 839 on a size 26 tapestry needle.

Main branches and large leaves

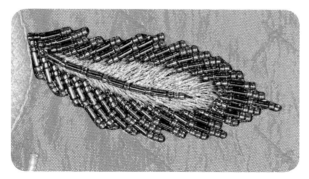

1. Thread one strand of 469 onto a size 10 bead embroidery needle. Double it over and tie the two ends together with a knot. Using this thread, bead-couch a row of beads onto each diagonal line that makes up the wide outer border of the petal. Come up on the outside edge. Pick up between 1 to 3 x 15°1527, 1 x #1.26 bugle and 2 to 3 x 15°197 beads. Vary the number of each of the beads according to the length of the line.

2. With 1 strand of *Fils Métallisé* 4052 on a size 7 embroidery needle, do a long straight stitch between the bead lines to create a slight sparkle.

3. Starting at the tip, with a straight stitch, fill the inside of each leaf with diagonal satin stitches. On each side, the stitches should start at the end of the

bead lines and finish on the line which forms the vein running up the middle of the leaf. Use 1 strand of koeksister thread 07 on a size 22 chenille needle.

4. Thread one strand of 469 onto a size 10 bead embroidery needle. Double it over and tie the two ends together with a knot. Using this thread, bead-couch a row of beads up the vein. Start at the base of the leaf with a 15°197 followed by a #1.26 bugle, alternating these two beads all the way up and finishing with 3 x 15°197 beads.

5. The three branches in the design are stitched in the same way.

6. Pad the stems with stem stitch using 3 strands of 3023.

7. Using 1 strand of the same thread, work diagonal satin stitch over the padding.

8. Using 1 strand of 3022 work a diagonal trellis over the stem. Create it in the same way that you would trellis by doing long straight stitches from edge. Unlike trellis couching, do not place a couching stitch at each intersection.

9. Using 1 strand of the same thread, outline each branch with fine stem stitch.

Stranded thread conversion charts

Whilst embroiderers will usually stitch with one brand of thread, different brands can be used together. Both DMC and Anchor are good quality threads and the only reason why one would use one in preference to the other is for its colour. Use these conversions as a guide only. They are the closest match and are, in many cases, not identical. If you are substituting one range for another, be careful that the colours work together, particularly when you are doing shading.

ANCHOR TO DMC

Anchor	DMC
68	3687
69	3803
70	814
72	154
1028	3685

DMC TO LIZBETH #80

DMC	Lizbeth #80
3052	684
397	631

DMC TO ANCHOR

DMC	Anchor	DMC	Anchor	DMC	Anchor
Ecru	926	772	1043	3052	859
152	894	777	43	3053	260
154	72	779	359	3607	87
155	1030	798	137	3609	85
221	1015	799	145	3685	972
223	895	800	159	3687	68
224	893	803	149	3688	1016
225	1026	809	130	3689	49
312	147	822	926	3722	1027
322	978	839	1050	3740	873
333	119	869	944	3743	869
334	977	924	851	3750	1036
340	118	926	850	3781	1050
422	373	927	849	3787	393
469	267	928	274	3790	898
520	861	930	922	3803	69
522	859	931	1034	3812	189
523	858	932	343	3828	890
524	858	934	269	3829	901
561	212	939	152	3831	42
562	208	958	187	3832	38
563	204	959	185	3833	1022
564	206	3011	924	3834	970
640	903	3012	855	3835	98
642	392	3013	854	3836	66
644	830	3021	905	3847	211
676	891	3022	1040	3848	205
677	886	3023	392	3849	849
712	926	3041	871	3860	903
738	942	3042	870	3861	899
739	1009	3051	268	3866	397

Buyer's guide

Five of the designs in this book have been designed for objects that are specifically manufactured for mounting embroidery. These are available online and the links for each object are listed below:

A Sherry For Jack
Devon Dresser Walnut Tray
www.herrschners.com/Product/
Devon+Dresser+Tray+FREE+Pattern.aspx

Pertinacity
Louis XV Carved Round Footstool
www.australianneedlearts.com.au/louis-xv-carved-round-footstool

Dancing Threads
Butterfly Garden Music Box
www.nordicneedle.com/prod/7470.html

Vyesna
Petite Mantel Clock #48111
www.sudberry.com/catalog/mantelclock.htm

No-Slip Hoops and Lap Stands
Morgan Hoops and Stands Inc.
http://www.nosliphoops.com/

Australian Needlearts (Australia)
http://www.australianneedlearts.com.au/morgan-lap-stands

Grip-n-Stitch Needlework Frame
Sew It All (UK and Europe)
www.sewitall.com/webshop/162-grip-or-clip-frame

Sew It All (Australia)
sewitall.com.au/shop/index.php?cPath=417

Yarn Tree (USA)
yarntree.com/cross-stitch/index.php?main_page=product_info&products_id=10862

In addition to the above Hazel Blomkamp has an active mail-order business for all fabric, thread and bead requisites related to her designs. Screen-printed fabric panels, bead packs and thread packs for all of the projects in this book are available from her website **www.hazelblomkamp.co.za**

It is possible that, from time to time, bead and thread colours are discontinued. If you are unable to find specific threads and beads for any of the projects in this book, please email Hazel at **info@hazelblomkamp.co.za** and she will be able to send requisites to you or, in the event that they have been discontinued, suggest viable alternatives.

Patterns

A sherry for Jack (p. 43)
Actual size: 225 mm ($8^{55}/_{64}$")
x 105 mm ($4^{9}/_{64}$")

Pertinacity (p. 57)
Actual size: 330 mm (13") diameter

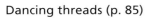

Dancing threads (p. 85)
Actual size: 120 mm (4¾″) x 77 mm (3″)

The first sip (p. 95)
Actual size: 260 mm (10¼")
x 200 mm (8") high

Vyesna Prishla (p. 109)
Actual size: 170 mm (6¾") x 116 mm (4½")

Inflorescence (p. 141)
Actual size: 110 mm (4⅓") x 211 mm (8⅓")

Actual size: 80 mm (3⅛") high

Late harvest (p. 119)
Actual size: 365 mm (14½") x 115 mm (4½")

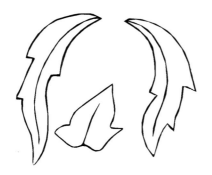

Centre fruit
Actual size: 59 mm (2⁵/₆") x 68 mm (2¹¹/₁₆")

Far left fruit
Actual size: 37 mm (1½") x 43 mm (1¹¹/₁₆")

Far right fruit
Actual size: 45 mm (1¹³/₁₆") x 51 mm (2")

Left top flower leaves
Actual size: 16 mm (⁵/₈") x 15 mm (⁹/₁₆")

Left large grape bunch leaves
Actual size: 20 mm (¹³/₁₆") x 22 mm (¹⁵/₁₆")

Small grape bunch leaves
Actual size: 12 mm (¹/₂") x 12 mm (¹/₂")

HAZEL *Blomkamp*

Hazel Blomkamp has dabbled with all the needlecrafts since childhood. When her children were babies she developed a passion for embroidery to break the tedium of life with toddlers, using it as her evening reward for having got through the day with her sanity intact. Her children are now young adults and she still embroiders in front of the television every night. She has been designing for the past 20 years. Preferring to design projects which appear to be traditional, she pushes the boundaries by introducing other forms of needlecraft into traditional techniques, exploring further in everything that she does. Along with designing, she runs a busy website from home. She teaches at her home studio, in Pietermaritzburg, KZN, and travels throughout South Africa and to Australia teaching embroidery and fine beadwork. She is a regular contributor to South African and Australian embroidery magazines and is a columnist for South African *Stitches* Magazine.